BRITISH
STEAM RAILWAYS

BRITISH
STEAM RAILWAYS

DAVID ROSS

p

This is a Parragon Book
This edition published in 2004

Parragon
Queen Street House
4 Queen Street
Bath BA1 1HE, UK

Copyright © Parragon 2002

Hardback ISBN 1-40541-643-2
Paperback ISBN 1-40543-730-8

Editorial and design by
Amber Books Ltd
Bradley's Close
74–77 White Lion Street
London N1 9PF

Printed in Dubai

Contents

1 · The Pioneering Years

A few short decades will see the railways grow into a major industry dominated by speculators and managers. But in the early days it is the engineers – among them George and Robert Stephenson, Isambard Kingdom Brunel and Joseph Locke – who are at the heart of the steam railway.

LEFT Stephenson's *Invicta*, the first locomotive to run in Kent, was shipped from Newcastle to Whitstable in 1830. Not a particularly successful engine, it was unable to cope with the gradients on the line. A failed attempt to sell it nine years later led to its storage and subsequent preservation.

OPPOSITE The restored Furness Railway 0-4-0 No 20 is Britain's oldest working locomotive, built in 1863. In 1870, it was sold to the local steelworks and converted to a saddle tank, working in this form until 1960. The Furness Railway Trust restored it to its original appearance, and it has been in steam again since January 1999.

BY THE YEAR 1804, the steam engine had already been a well-known and accepted fact of industrial life for several decades. A few inventive pioneers had succeeded in driving ships with it. But on land, it had always been fixed in one place, driving pumps or other machinery. No self-propelling steam engine had ever run on land. Then, in February 1804, the owner of Penydarren Ironworks, in South Wales, made a hefty bet with a local rival. He wagered the sum of 500 guineas that a steam-powered 'travelling engine', set up on his mining tramroad by the Cornish engineer Richard Trevithick, would pull a load of 10 tons (10.16 tonnes) from Penydarren to Abercynon, a distance of just under 10 miles (16km). The bet was taken. The locomotive, first in the world to run on rails, made the journey in 4 hours 5 minutes, with 70 men clinging on to the wagons, which

LEFT *Puffing Billy*, built by William Hedley and Christopher Blackett for the Wylam Colliery in Northumberland in 1813, had a rocking-beam drive, transmitting power via cog-wheels to the four driving wheels, and was among the first engines to have exhaust steam directed through the long chimney.

were loaded with pig iron. The brittle, flanged cast-iron track was broken and cracked by the engine's wheels, however, and Penydarren went back to pony-hauling for 30 years. But that day, on a bleak Welsh plateau, the steam railway was born.

Twenty-one years later, it came of age. On 27 September 1825, the Stockton & Darlington Railway opened for business, the first public steam-powered railway in the world. In 1830, it was followed by the Liverpool & Manchester. With its great

BELOW In July 1925, the centenary of the world's first public railway, the Stockton & Darlington, was celebrated by a number of events mounted by the ever publicity-conscious LNER, including this re-enactment of the first train, drawn by a replica of *Locomotion*.

embankment across Chat Moss and the imposing Sankey Viaduct, this line showed how railways would slice through the landscape. Linking two fast-growing industrial cities, it also showed how railways would bring a revolutionary change to inland transport. Although its opening was marred by the death of the politician William Huskisson – ironically, an enthusiastic supporter of railways and the first victim of a railway accident – the progress of railways was unstoppable.

EXPERIENCE, THE BEST TEACHER

There was a great deal to learn, and no one to teach it. The first generation of railwaymen had to make up the rule book, and the technical handbooks, as they went along. One of the reasons the first railway engineers avoided all but the gentlest of gradients was that no one knew how effective the adhesion of an iron driving wheel, on an iron rail, would be on a rising grade. Locomotive building was still in its infancy.

Before the Liverpool & Manchester opened, a set of trials was held at Rainhill in October 1829 to determine the type of engine that would be used on the line. A prize of £500 was offered for the one which best satisfied the conditions laid down. Timothy Hackworth, engineer of the Stockton & Darlington, entered his *Sans Pareil*, and two other designers also competed. The competition was won with ease by Robert Stephenson's locomotive *Rocket*, which was in fact the only competitor to stay the course.

By this time, a number of technical problems had been solved. Trevithick had developed the flanged wheel, to run on a flat rail, in 1805. George Stephenson (father of Robert), whose engine-building business began in 1814, improved on the blast system that drew steam through the boiler; with his colleague Henry Booth he also devised the multi-tube boiler.

0-4-0 LOCOMOTION S&D 1825	
Tractive effort: 1900lb (862kg)	
Axle load: 4704lb (2.13 tonnes)	
Cylinders: two 9½x24in (241x609mm)	
Driving wheels: 48in (122cm)	
Heating surface: 60sq ft (5.6m²)	
Superheater: n/a	
Steam pressure: 50psi (3.5kg/cm²)	
Grate area: 8sq ft (0.74m2)	
Fuel: Coke – 2200lb (1 tonne)	
Water: 400gall (480 US) (1.8m³)	
Total weight: 15,232lb (6.9 tonnes)	
Overall length: 10ft 4in (3.15m)	

ABOVE *Locomotion*, built by George Stephenson, was the first engine to operate on a public railway – between Stockton and Darlington – on 25 September 1825. It was also the first to have its wheels linked by coupling rods, but was soon to be superseded by more powerful and less fragile types.

Rocket had amazed and alarmed spectators by reaching 29mph, but it was soon eclipsed by a new model from the same designer. This engine, *Planet*, further developed in *Patentee* of 1837, showed the shape of things to come; indeed, its basic design remained that of all British steam locomotives for more than a hundred years. Unlike all previous engines, whose cylinders drove the pistons from above or behind, *Planet*'s cylinders were in front, tucked beneath the smoke-box and inside the frame.

A minor but very public attribute of each locomotive was its name. In these early years, a 'class' of engines was hardly thought of; each was an individual, with improvements on its predecessor, and a name was deemed to be the best identifier. The tradition of naming engines, which goes back to their very beginning, would be continued by most British lines.

In its first year, the Liverpool & Manchester Railway carried 460,000 passengers. This was more than four times the previous number of travellers between the two cities. For both business and pleasure, the railway opened up new opportuni-ties. From the first, animals were carried, as well as people and freight. Just as the first

0-2-2 ROCKET L&MR 1829

Tractive effort: 2405lb (1089kg)
Axle load: 5600lb (2.54 tonnes)
Cylinders: two 8x17in (203x432mm)
Driving wheels: 56½in (143.5cm)
Heating surface: 117.75sq ft (10.9m²)
Superheater: n/a
Steam pressure: 50psi (3.52kg/cm²)
Grate area: 8sq ft (0.74m²)
Fuel: Coke – 2200lb (1 tonne)
Water: 400gall (480 US) (1.8m³)
Total weight: 9520lb (4.32 tonnes)
Overall length: 7ft 2in (2.18m)

railway carriages simply reproduced the form of the road coach, so goods wagons copied the side-loading farm cart – as also did the cheapest passenger vehicles, which possessed neither roof nor seats. Luggage was carried stage-coach-style, on the roofs of carriages.

The success of these Northern lines was noted in the South. Even in 1824, a line had been planned between Canterbury and Whitstable, in Kent, replacing a plan for a canal. It was opened in 1830 and its first engine, *Invicta*, was sent down from Newcastle by sea. The Leicester & Swannington, in the Midlands, was opened in 1832. Another early line was in Cornwall, Trevithick's home county, between Bodmin and Wadebridge in 1834. Other short lines opened elsewhere, sometimes to be incorporated into main trunk lines later on. But for the engineers – and for investors, who were beginning to get interested in the money-making potential of railway companies – the great prize was London, the biggest city in the world. The capital's first railway was the London & Greenwich, with its terminus at London Bridge. The tracks were carried all the way on a brick viaduct, which set the pattern for other South London lines. The heyday of the commuter line was still some way off, and the promoters' eyes – in this first, relatively mild outburst of 'railway mania' – were mainly on trunk routes from the capital.

BELOW *Northumbrian*, which was built by Stephenson in 1830, less than a year after *Rocket*, embodied many improvements, including a smoke-box, horizontal cylinders and a boiler incorporating water-space around the firebox – all fundamentals of locomotive design. It also had what was probably the first true tender.

GIANTS OF THE EARLY DAYS

The great men of the early railway were not in fact the promoters or managers, but the engineers. Among these were the towering figures of George Stephenson and his son

2-2-0 PLANET L&MR 1830

Tractive effort: 1371lb (622kg)

Axle load: 6720lb (3 tonnes)

Cylinders: two 11x16in (279x406mm)

Driving wheels: 60in (152.5cm)

Heating surface: not known

Superheater: n/a

Steam pressure: 50psi (3.52kg/cm²)

Grate area: 8sq ft (0.74m²)

Fuel: Coke – 2200lb (1 tonne)

Water: not known

Total weight: 17,920lb (8 tonnes)

Overall length: 9ft 6in (2.9m)

Robert. George had begun as a working man in the collieries of the North-East. An interest in engines, and his own drive and energy, made him into first a mechanic, then an engineer. The intelligence, common sense and determination of George Stephenson underlay the success of the Liverpool & Manchester Railway. The design both of its bold permanent way and of its locomotives set the pattern that others would follow. Robert Stephenson inherited his father's gifts as both a civil and a mechanical engineer. As new railway schemes were proposed, the developers

ABOVE A modern replica of the first of the 2-2-2 'Planet' class, shown here at Loughborough on the Great Central Railway in 1993. The wood-lined boiler can clearly be seen. The cylinders are set under the smoke-box, inside the frames, a practice which would continue to be common in British locomotive design.

would inevitably come to the Stephensons, or to one of the engineers whom they had trained. It was not only their expertise that was wanted; their very names spelt success to potential investors. It would be George Stephenson's immense personal authority, as much as anything else, that later won the so-called 'Battle of the Gauges'.

The first of the great trunk lines was the one which linked London to Birmingham, Manchester and Liverpool. It began in the North with the Grand Junction Railway, running from Birmingham to join the Liverpool–Manchester line at Warrington. Its engineer was Joseph Locke, another of the giants of the early railway age. He had been trained by George Stephenson, though later he and the Stephensons became rivals, with no love lost between them. At this time there was no great distinction between the branches of engineering – the same man might design and lay out the line and also design the locomotives which ran on it (sometimes with unfortunate results). Locke, however, stuck to the civil engineering side, and he employed locomotive engineers. A vital contribution from him was the development of a heavier, 'double-headed' rail in 1835, allowing for heavier trains and a greater axle-loading on the engines. The engineering contractor for the Grand Junction line was another notable figure, Thomas Brassey, who was to become the greatest railway contractor in the world, laying tracks as far away as Russia, and often managing the lines he built. In Britain alone, Brassey's company laid 1700 miles (2736km) of railway.

South of Birmingham, the London & Birmingham line was engineered by Robert Stephenson. The Grand Junction opened on 4 July 1837, and the London & Birmingham followed on 9 April 1838. Its opening had been delayed by the digging of Kilsby Tunnel, 2400yds (2.19km) long, just south of Rugby, where unexpected underground springs had caused massive problems. Its eventual cost was more than three times the estimate of £99,000. The line's London terminus was at Euston Square.

BELOW The elevated Blackfriars Station, looking north across the Thames in 1863. The link via Blackfriars to the Great Northern at King's Cross had a strategic potential that remained undeveloped beyond suburban services.

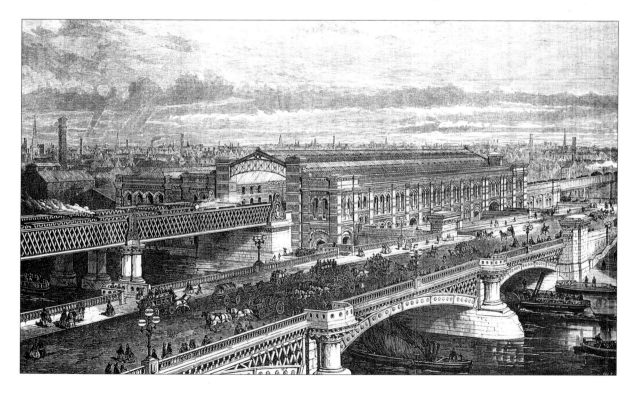

Trains made a refreshment pause at Wolverton, where later a locomotive and carriage works would be set up.

With these long lines, and the cuttings and embankments they needed, emerged the nomadic army of navvies (the name, from 'navigators', shows how they began as canal diggers). Part of Brassey's genius was in the management of these strong and frequently unruly men (a day's work for one of them was reckoned as the equivalent of hoisting 20 tons (20,321kg) of earth to a height of 6ft/1.83m). The shanty towns where they lived attracted all kinds of merchants, con men and entertainers of various sorts.

BRUNEL, MAN OF VISION

The trunk-route map of 1838 looked like a wobbly T with a narrow top bar, but already its shape was changing. As early as 1832, a group of Bristol merchants put forward a plan for a London-to-Bristol line. They employed a 27-year-old engineer, Isambard Kingdom Brunel, son of an immigrant French engineer, who already had experience of tunnelling beneath the Thames and was known in Bristol for his design of the Clifton Suspension Bridge over the River Avon. The board's plan had been to appoint the man who gave the lowest estimate, but Brunel roundly told them that this would be a disaster and that he would withdraw his application if they maintained this policy. The board caved in, and he was appointed. From then on, Brunel was the moving spirit of the railway.

His concept for the line, already known as the Great Western Railway, was on the grand scale. Its gauge was to be, not Stephenson's 4ft 8½in (1.435m), which was based on the old colliery tramways, but 7ft ¼in (2.14m). Instead of being laid on transverse sleepers, it was laid on long baulks placed underneath the rails. In a few weeks of hectic

ABOVE Isambard Kingdom Brunel (1806–59) was an engineer of genius who liked to operate on the grand scale. It was he who decreed the broad gauge to which the original Great Western Railway was built. His vision was of a London–New York service, in which passengers would transfer at Bristol from magnificent trains on to magnificent steamships – all of his own design.

LEFT The coats of arms of the Cities of London and Bristol are linked in the arms of the Great Western Railway, reminders of the Committees in each place which together founded the company.

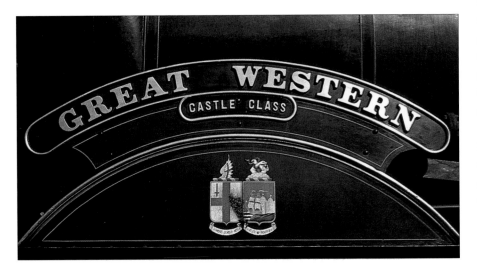

activity, the line was surveyed. A 1.8-mile (2.9km) tunnel was planned to cut through the limestone ridge at Box, east of Bath. Because this was to be built on a grade of one in 100, regarded by many as impossible to climb, there was a great public outcry, whipped up by such vocal opponents of the railway as Dr Dionysus Lardner, who also claimed that, if the brakes failed going downhill, the train would come out of the tunnel at 120mph (193km/h). It took until 1835 to get Parliamentary approval to build the line, and the works were not completed until 30 June 1841.

By this time, a line from Bristol to Exeter was also under construction further west. As on the Birmingham line, a central spot was chosen for a refreshment stop and engine-changing. This was Swindon. Engine-changing proved unnecessary, but the refreshment stop was traditional for decades. It was a profit source to the company, which received a high rent from caterers, who in turn charged inflated prices for indifferent fare. Brunel wrote: 'I have long ceased to make complaints about Swindon. I avoid taking anything there when I can help it.'

Brunel had original ideas about everything, but not all of them worked in practice. The locomotive designs for the new railway proved hopelessly inefficient and unreliable. Fortunately he had hired a young mechanical engineer trained by the Stephensons, Daniel Gooch. The 20-year-old Gooch had a nightmare task in getting Brunel's huge-wheeled and underpowered machines to work, but eventually his own designs would make the Great Western the fastest and most punctual of all the early lines.

ABOVE A distinguished veteran, this well-tank 2-4-0T was designed by Joseph Beattie for the London & South Western Railway in 1863 and built in 1874. With two companions, it survived on the Bodmin–Wadebridge line in Cornwall into the 1950s, although it acquired a new boiler more than once during its long life.

The next port to be joined to London was Southampton, via the London & Southampton Railway (renamed London and South-Western Railway from 1839). Engineered by Joseph Locke, it cut through the downs in steep cuttings, with minimal tunnelling, and crossed valleys on lofty embankments. It was opened in stages and completed on 11 May 1840. At that time Southampton was not a major seaport, and it was perhaps surprising that Portsmouth, the country's chief naval base, was not selected as a terminus. But the British government, unlike those of some other countries, took no part in planning the rail network. Instead, new schemes were promoted by the businessmen and industrialists of individual towns. It was the railway which made Southampton into a major transatlantic seaport. Later, too, the LSWR would be an efficient carrier of large numbers, but its first effort – to take racegoers to the Derby at Epsom in 1838 – caused a riot when far too many people tried to board the race-day specials at its Nine Elms terminus (Waterloo would not become the London terminus for another 10 years).

LEFT A distinctive feature of the Newcastle–Carlisle line is its lofty, jettied signal boxes, which give the signalman an especially good view of approaching trains. This one is at Haltwhistle.

OPPOSITE A Bristol-bound local train drawn by a Great Western tank locomotive approaches Box Tunnel, once described by an opponent of railways as 'monstrous, extraordinary, most dangerous and impractible'.

BELOW The GWR's first Great Western, Daniel Gooch's 4-2-2 design of 1846, embodied most of the features of his broad-gauge engines to come. In size, power and performance, it outclassed any locomotive then in existence.

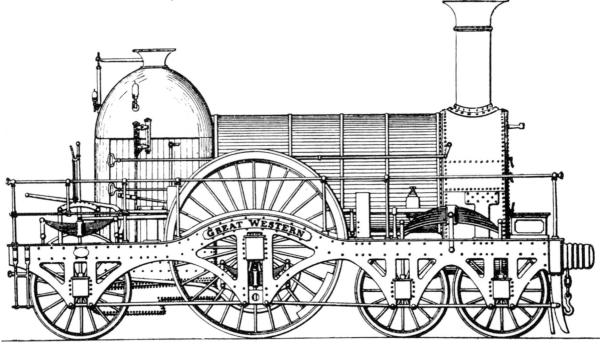

By 1839, the first east–west cross-country line was completed, the Newcastle & Carlisle. With its main purpose being to transport iron ore from Cumberland to the Tyne, it made a regular and handsome profit. It was on this line that a ticket clerk, Thomas Edmondson, invented the ticket-printing machine, which remained standard on all lines for many decades and made him a rich man.

CONTROL UNDER THE BOARD OF TRADE

In 1844, with schemes for new railways arising all over the country, the government made an effort to control the development of railways and to regulate existing companies. The Board of Trade, led by its president, William Ewart Gladstone, aimed to bring some strategic vision into the piecemeal and competitive proposals for new railway lines. This was fiercely resisted by the companies, which were among the first to employ what today would be known as PR consultants. The main result was the 'Parliamentary train': every company had to run at least one daily train conveying third-class passengers, 'in carriages provided with seats and protected from the weather', at a speed not less than 12mph (19.3km/h) and at a fare of a penny a mile for adults. This compulsory service was often provided grudgingly and at extremely unsociable hours. The railway companies were interested in the 'carriage trade', first- and

ABOVE Track-laying was a labour-intensive activity, as this 1930s painting by Stanhope Forbes, R.A., shows. Each section of track was maintained by a separate 'gang', but bigger teams combined for the heavy work of laying new track-lengths. Rail weights more than doubled between the 1830s and 1870s.

second-class passengers, who paid the full fare. The Board of Trade remained the government body responsible for railways, but it played no part in determining their progress.

In the early 1840s, many people felt that the country by now had all the railway lines it really needed. In fact, a huge expansion of railway planning and building was about to take place. This was the 'Railway Mania', which raged in 1845–46. It had several causes. One was the failure of the government to achieve control over railway development. Others were the increasing reliability of rail technology and the growth of public acceptance of the new transport medium.

But the chief cause of the mania was greed, which operated at various levels of the social scale. At one end, it brought in rich men such as George Hudson, a former Lord Mayor of York, who saw opportunities in railway management to get much richer. At the other end, many ordinary individuals borrowed money to buy shares in new companies, which they then immediately sold at a profit, in order to buy even more shares in other companies. To secure shares, only a 10 per cent deposit was necessary, with the balance to be called up later. When

ABOVE The LNWR coopted Britannia and her lion onto its coat of arms. The companies liked florid heraldry, and their emblems could be found on every kind of equipment, from cast-iron platform seats to crockery in the restaurant cars, as well as locomotives (see next page).

LEFT The preserved Furness Railway 0-4-0 No 3, *Coppernob*, a goods engine designed by William Bury and built in 1846, is a more substantial machine than the lightweight types built by Bury for the London & Birmingham Railway. It shows his typical bar-frame construction (frames inside the wheels).

the companies came to call up this balance, the shareholders were often unable to pay. In the middle, many well-off people invested heavily in what their financial advisers assured them was a bonanza.

As more and more new companies were formed, the existing ones tried to fight them off by building new lines, often with no other intention than to block rivals' plans. Railway shares, selling at completely unrealistic prices, were the equivalent of the dot.com shares of the first years of the twenty-first century. In 1845–46, 6710 miles (10,798km) of new railway were authorized, including extensive mileage in Scotland and Wales. More than 1200 new companies put forward schemes, at an estimated total cost of more than £500,000,000 – a colossal sum even for a fast-growing industrial economy.

The crash was inevitable. Much of the promised capital investment was non-existent. Many companies collapsed even before their schemes were approved. Others got approval, but had no money to proceed. Thousands of people were ruined, and a special body had to be set up to deal with the

BELOW The fine paintwork of the 1890s is shown off in this detail of a class T3 express engine of the London & South-Western Railway.

problems of lines which had Parliamentary approval, but no funds to complete, or sometimes even to begin, the work.

There were sound business reasons for getting an Act of Parliament to promote a railway. Most importantly, it gave the company compulsory purchase powers to get the necessary ground, albeit at a fair price. While towns were glad to get railways, rich landowners often strongly resisted. The London & Birmingham Railway avoided the important town of Northampton, despite the town's enthusiasm to be on the line, mainly because the owners of the land around the town created so many difficulties. A loop eventually linked Northampton to the main line in 1875.

FORMATION OF THE GREAT COMPANIES

For those railway companies which survived the mania, the worst effect was to make them jealous and mistrustful of one another. The growing complexity of the system had already made it necessary, in 1842, to establish the Railway Clearing House, a central office which recorded all movement of goods and passengers through the system from company to company, allocating the routes taken and the correct share of the carriage cost to each one. Membership was voluntary, and it was not until 1865 that the majority were linked in. Beginning with a staff of six clerks, it would have almost 3000 employees by 1910. Its annual handbook was an indispensable volume for anyone in the transport business. The Clearing House was almost the sole example of cooperation, other than when the companies banded together to resist any new efforts at government 'interference'.

Through the troubled years of the mania and the more cautious time that followed, the main arteries of the rail system became clear. The great companies that would gradually dominate the scene were being formed. In October 1848, the London & Birmingham, Grand Junction and Liverpool & Manchester amalgamated to form the London & North Western Railway, which would proudly call itself the 'Premier Line'. The Midland Railway was formed in May 1844 out of a cluster of lines between Birmingham and Derby. After overcoming intense opposition from the Midland and the London & Birmingham, the Great Northern Railway was established in May 1846, running in a direct line from London to York. With the Great Western and the London & South Western, these lines held the central ground. In between, and to east and west, were dozens of other companies, most destined to be swallowed up eventually by one of the titans. Only in the South-East of England were there lines which remained outside their net.

The most prominent railway figure at this time was George Hudson, nicknamed the Railway King,

OPPOSITE The elegant left-hand driver of F.W. Webb's celebrated 1874 'Precedent' class 2-4-0 Hardwicke, built by the LNWR at Crewe, and one of the participants in the great Race to the North of 1895. The opening in the wheel-splasher is not just for aesthetics: it provides a space via which the inside axle-box can be lubricated.

THE BRITISH RAILWAY
SYSTEM IN 1842

the first non-engineer to achieve national fame through the railways. Hudson was involved with a great number of lines, mostly between the Midlands and York and in the North-East, but also with the Eastern Counties Railway, which ran from London to East Anglia and had hopes of extending northwards to York and so providing an East Coast London–Edinburgh service. Hudson, through his involvement with the Midland Railway and the Eastern Counties, and also with the York–Newcastle–Berwick line, coordinated virulent opposition to the Great Northern's plans for a direct London–York line. Then, in 1848, Hudson, who controlled the little York & North Midland line, made a deal with the Great Northern, allowing GN trains to use his line from Burton Salmon, just north of Doncaster, into York, rather than make its own line (at this time the GN was extremely short of money). Although a director of the Midland and the Eastern Counties Railways, Hudson had made a private arrangement with an 'enemy' line for his own benefit. Up to then, there had been subdued murmurs against his business practices, but now critics became more vocal. Committees of board members and shareholders began to examine the accounts of Hudson-managed companies and found all kinds of evidence of illegal share-dealing and manipulation of the accounts. By 1849, the former Railway King had fallen into disgrace.

In 1848, it became possible to travel by train from London to Glasgow following the completion of the Lancaster & Carlisle Railway and the Caledonian main line through the Clyde and Annan valleys. These lines, in British terms at least, were mountain ones, topping summits of almost 1000ft (304m) at Shap and 1014ft (309m) at

ABOVE A portrait of George Hudson (1800–71) in his prime. Something comes through of the truculence and confidence, as well as the self-importance, of the great railway promoter. In his hand, no doubt, is another prospectus for a line which cannot fail to make its shareholders' fortunes.

LEFT Few people in history have built themselves such a memorial as I.K. Brunel's Saltash bridge over the Tamar, finished just before his death in 1859 and completing the mainline connection from Paddington to Penzance. The main tubular/suspension spans are each 455ft (138m) long.

Beattock. At Beattock and Tebay stations, banking engines were kept into the 1960s to help push heavy trains up the grades. The establishment of the West Coast route into Scotland spurred on the East Coast interests. They had no mountains, but two water gaps over the Tyne and the Tweed, bridged by Robert Stephenson's High Level Tyne Bridge in 1850 and the Royal Border Bridge at Berwick-upon-Tweed in 1849, the year in which through services from London to Edinburgh began. A more formidable gap was bridged in 1850 by Robert Stephenson's Britannia tubular iron bridge across the Menai Strait, completing the Irish Mail route between London and Holyhead. In 1859, a further spectacular bridge was completed, Brunel's last great achievement, the Royal Albert Bridge over the Tamar estuary at Saltash. He died soon after it was finished.

The up-and-over technique of the West Coast line was less feasible with trans-Pennine routes. Lengthy tunnels were dug to link the manufacturing districts to east and west of the backbone of England. In 1845, the Woodhead Tunnel, between

ABOVE Robert Stephenson's Royal Border Bridge of 1849 displays the quality of the best Victorian engineering. More than a hundred years later, in 1954, LNER class A4 4-6-2 *Golden Plover* takes a northbound express off the bridge and into the station at Berwick-upon-Tweed.

23

Manchester and Sheffield, was opened, longest in the world at 3 miles and 22 yards (4.85km); in 1850, it was pipped by the Standedge Tunnel, just 35 yards (32m) longer.

STATION DESIGN ON A GRAND SCALE

By mid-century, some of the great stations were established in a form still recognizable today, such as Newcastle Central, built in 1850–51, and York. Brunel's original building at Bristol Temple Meads still stands, though reduced to being a car park. In London, several great terminal stations were established by 1854, including Euston, Paddington (rebuilt by Brunel and Wyatt in 1854), King's Cross, Liverpool Street and London Bridge. Engineer-architects created these buildings; one of them, Lewis Cubitt, designer of King's Cross (first much criticized and later much admired for its 'plainness'), had also laid out the Great Northern line.

Railway architecture was often designed to reassure the inexperienced and anxious traveller. The great Doric arch at the entrance to Euston deliberately recalled the triumphal arch at the end of a great Roman road. Every style of architecture was used in station building. Some were grand – Hereford had a sort of Tudor mansion, while Kidderminster an imitation half-timbered Elizabethan house – but many lines, such as the South Eastern, could only afford 'temporary' wooden sheds, which often lasted a very long time. Builders had to resolve new problems, such as the ventilation of engine sheds. The first roundhouse was built at Derby in 1840. Much use was made of new material such as wrought and cast iron. Vast, curving aisled halls such as that of

ABOVE Deliberately imitating the great arches at the ends of Roman roads, the London & Birmingham Railway's classical-style gateway to Euston Station. Designed by Philip Hardwick, it was intended to reassure anxious passengers. It was pulled down in 1966 prior to the building of the new Euston.

OPPOSITE The original train shed at Temple Meads Station, Bristol, designed by I.K. Brunel and built in 1841. The central tracks of termini such as this were used as carriage sidings, until traffic expansion required additional platforms.

LEFT The original Britannia bridge across the Menai Strait, designed by Robert Stephenson and William Fairbairn, built in 1850 and completing the Irish Mail route from Euston to Holyhead. After a fire in 1970, it was rebuilt on steel arches, reopening in 1972.

York Station were completely new in architecture. In 25 years from the opening of the Stockton & Darlington, the railways had come to express a proud confidence in the newly invented business of mass transport of goods and people.

This confidence was based on considerable improvements in the power and reliability of that most vital feature, the locomotive. By 1850, the engines of the early years were obsolete, and the survival of even a handful is remarkable. The Planet type had established the basic layout and components, but many improvements of detail were made, and there was a steady increase in size, weight and tractive effort. Some lines designed their own engines from the start. The Liverpool & Manchester benefited from Robert Stephenson's, while the young Great Western suffered from Brunel's.

Locomotive works were already established to build engines for collieries. They built to each designer's specification or supplied their own models, as required. Bury, Curtis and Kennedy supplied the engines for

BELOW A modern view of York Station, designed by Thomas Prosser and built in 1877. The curving nave was without precedent in conventional architecture.

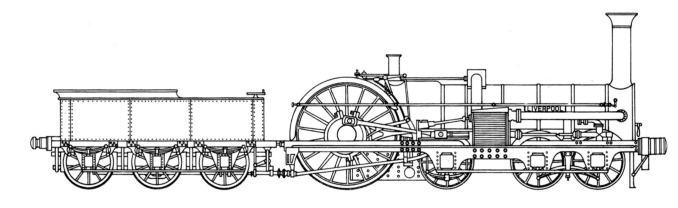

6-2-0 LIVERPOOL LNWR 1848

Tractive effort: 5700lb (2585kg)
Axle load: 26,208lb (11.9 tonnes)
Cylinders: two 18x20in (457x508mm)
Driving wheels: 96in (243.8cm)
Heating surface: 1529sq ft (142m²)
Superheater: n/a
Steam pressure: 100psi (7.05kg/cm²)
Grate area: 16sq ft (1.48 m²)
Fuel: Coke
Water: 1600gall (1921 US) (7.3m³)
Total weight: 57,344lb (26 tonnes)
Overall length: 18ft 6in (5.6m)

the London & Birmingham line and became notorious for their lack of innovation. Their answer to demands for greater power was simply to supply more of their little 2-2-0 four-wheeler engines, of which as many as four might be attached to a single train. Eventually their contract was terminated. Other builders were more enterprising, including Robert Stephenson's own company, also E.B. Wilson of Leeds, and Sharp, Roberts of Manchester, though there was still a degree of trial-and-error in design and construction.

Each railway company had to set up workshops for maintenance and repair, and soon also for building. The Grand Junction moved its works from Edge Hill in Liverpool to the greenfield site of Crewe in 1843. The Great Western started the growth of Swindon in the same way in 1840. Doncaster became the home of the Great Northern's 'Plant' in 1853, more than doubling its population. These places were company towns where everything was owned by the railway. Even the vicar of Crewe was appointed by the head of the locomotive works (Francis Webb just happened to appoint his own brother).

SMALL IS BEAUTIFUL

British steam locomotives have always been considered relatively small compared to those of other countries. The main reason is the tight loading gauge, self-imposed by the first builders – Brunel excepted – for operating reasons. The first engines were built to run on tightly curving tracks in the narrow confines of collieries and factory yards. Later, when overbridges and tunnels were necessary, the smaller the required height and width, the cheaper the construction.

ABOVE Thomas Russell Crampton (1816–88) patented his rear-drive locomotive, *Liverpool*, in 1843.

BELOW On the completion of the East Coast main line between London and Edinburgh in 1850, the Great Northern Railway elaborated its already gaudy heraldic design by including the Scottish thistle and English rose – united by railway.

Designers had to excel in getting the maximum amount of steam from a boiler which, even in the twentieth century, could be hardly more than 6ft (1.83m) in diameter.

The first trains were very lightweight, especially the passenger trains. For these, the single-driver 2-2-2 engine was the most common motive power. For freight, the 2-4-0 and the longer-lasting 0-6-0 (with smaller driving wheels, but more of them) were the rule. The frame – the basic body structure supporting the boiler and resting on the axles – could be inside or outside the wheels; usually, except on the Great Western, it was inside. According to the designer's choice, the cylinders might be inside the frame, invisibly driving a crank axle, or outside, with connecting rods exposed. From early on, there was a preference for inside cylinders and the apparently effortless effect of movement they made. A Scottish engineer, Patrick Stirling, scornfully likened an outside-cylinder engine to 'a laddie running with his breeks down'.

Incidentally, these early locomotives were not great polluters. Most burned coke and made little smoke. Each main depot had coking ovens, to convert the coal into coke before it was used to fire the engines. The locomotives themselves were brightly

BELOW In 1863, the world's first underground railway, the Metropolitan, opened in London. Cut-and-cover tunnelling was the method used, seen here in an engraving of 1868, showing navvies hard at work digging out the junction at Baker Street for the Uxbridge line.

painted in the company's livery and usually embellished with copper domes and fittings. They were kept in a state of high polish. Often the engine driver ran his machine under contract to the company, himself paying the fireman and cleaners.

INFLUENTIAL ENGINEERS

Through the 1840s and 1850s, the job of mechanical engineer became steadily more specialized, and, with the work of construction of the line largely done, he became the company's most important non-administrative officer and very often a law unto himself. Significant design improvements were made, such as William Fernihough's use of balancing weights on the driving wheels to counterbalance the cranks. This innovation, on the Eastern Counties line, soon became universal. Engines began to be more substantially built and they lasted longer. Some of Daniel Gooch's single-drivers of 1840 lasted until the 1870s, though they acquired new boilers in the 1850s. (The process of cannibalization began early, whereby an apparently new locomotive might contain much of various predecessors. Rebuilds were frequent, and sometimes fictional, all designed to avoid incurring the capital cost of a completely new machine.)

Gooch was probably the most influential locomotive man of the mid-century. His achievement was based on providing engines with ample boilers, with steam pressure at 100psi (7.05kg/cm^2), which was standard for the time. Their performance was outstanding. His *Great Western* 2-2-2 of 1846 ran from Paddington to Swindon at almost

ABOVE In 1863, Archibald Sturrock designed a steam-tender 0-6-0 for the GNR, with an auxiliary engine driving the six tender wheels. It was unpopular with the crews and was removed when his successor rebuilt the engines, as seen here.

BELOW The GWR 4-2-2 *Iron Duke*, built in 1847, represents Daniel Gooch's standard express type. This would remain the basic traction of GW mainline services until the abolition of the broad gauge in 1892.

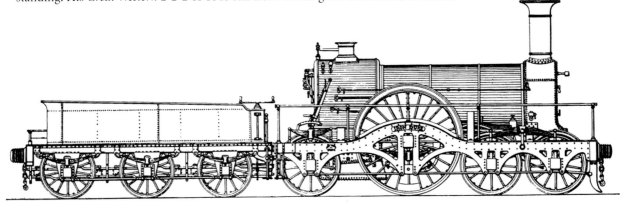

a mile a minute with a 100-ton (101.6-tonne) train in June of that year. Gooch also introduced scientific testing of locomotives, using a dynamometer car the equipment of which could measure the speed and power output. It was thought that such achievements were only possible on the broad gauge until one of Gooch's trainees, Archibald Sturrock, brought what he had learned to the Great Northern.

Sturrock, a Scot, was keen to speed up the East Coast route, and in 1853 he built a 4-2-2 express engine. Unlike previous British express types, the front four wheels were a bogie – prior to this, most engines had been on a rigid wheelbase with no pivoting wheels. But this 4-2-2 was a one-off: the time for racing to the North was not yet come, and Sturrock's other express engines were 2-4-0s and 2-2-2s, though with the very high boiler pressure of 150lb (68kg) and with fireboxes twice the size of anything that had gone before on the 'standard' gauge. Sturrock also designed a steam tender for his 0-6-0 freight engines, with steam piped to auxiliary cylinders which drove the tender wheels.

Another able designer, John Gray, was the inspiration behind the highly successful 'Jenny Lind' 2-2-2 type, built by E.B. Wilson's Railway Foundry at Leeds, which ran

ABOVE No broad-gauge locomotive has been preserved, but this view of a replica of *Iron Duke*, under steam, gives an indication of their imposing appearance. Even as mid-century approached, and speeds of up to 60mph (96km/h) became common, the enginemen were denied a cab.

2-2-2 BLOOMER LNWR 1851

Tractive effort: 8500lb (3854lb)
Axle load: 27,664lb (12.5 tonnes)
Cylinders: two 16x22in (406x558mm)
Driving wheels: 84in (213cm)
Heating surface: 1448.5sq ft (106.6m²)
Superheater: n/a
Steam pressure: 150psi (10.57kg/cm²)
Grate area: not known
Fuel: Coke/coal
Water: 1600gall (1,921 US) (7.3m³)
Total weight: 66,080lb (29.9 tonnes)
Overall length: 18ft 10in (5.74m)

first on the London Brighton & South Coast line in 1847. Gray demonstrated that boilers could be mounted high above the wheels without making the engines prone to capsize. Among other major developments of the 1850s was that by Charles Markham on the Midland Railway: a big firebox which efficiently burned bituminous coal was achieved by building an arch of fire-brick across the leading end. The coke ovens speedily disappeared.

Up to 1861, the LNWR built locomotives at both Crewe and Wolverton, for its northern and southern sections, as if the Grand Junction and London & Birmingham were still separate companies. The chief at Wolverton from 1849–61 was J.E. McConnell, famous for his 'Big Bloomers' introduced in 1851 (their nickname coming from Mrs Amelia Bloomer, a pioneer of ladies' trousering). Still with 2-2-2 wheel arrangement, the Bloomers followed Gray's example in having a high-set boiler, with the then very high pressure of 150psi (10.57kg/cm²). McConnell also designed the basic form of six-wheeled tender used by most other engine designers to replace the original, inadequate four-wheeled water-cart

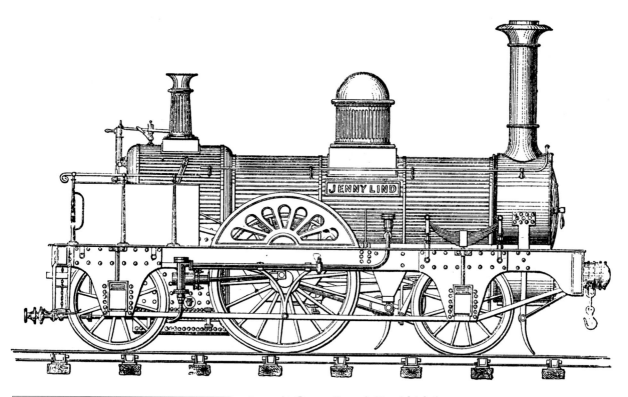

0-2-2 JENNY LIND 1847

Tractive effort: 6300lb (2857kg)
Axle load: 22,400lb (10.15 tonnes)
Cylinders: two 15x20in (381x508mm)
Driving wheels: 72in (183cm)
Heating surface: 800sq ft (74.3m²)
Superheater: n/a
Steam pressure: 120psi (8.46kg/cm²)
Grate area: not known
Fuel: Coke
Water: 1600gall (1921 US) (7.3m³)
Total weight: 53,760lb (24.4 tonnes)
Overall length: 13ft 6in (4.12m)

type. At Crewe, Francis Trevithick (son of locomotive pioneer Richard) was in charge when its first locomotive, the 2-2-2 *Columbine*, appeared in 1845. Many designers, notably Joseph Beattie on the London & South Western, tried their hand at improvements, often with an eye on royalties from patents, but the most successful engines were invariably those least festooned with such gadgets as feedwater heaters or double fireboxes (which burned coke in front and coal behind).

Surprisingly perhaps, the first 25 years of railway operation saw the introduction of many aspects which are more familiar from later years. The Grand Junction had a 'bed-carriage' which anticipated the sleeping car. The first Travelling Post Office was introduced on the same line in 1838, using a converted horsebox as a sorting carrriage, and in the same year the automatic pick-up of mail bags from the lineside was introduced. Organized excursion traffic began in 1841 with Thomas Cook's temperance picnic outing from Leicester to Loughborough – the first venture in what became an international business – and received a powerful boost from the Great Exhibition of 1851. Great improvement was made to the rails themselves and to the permanent way. Brunel's baulk road, rigidly fixed into the ground by log piles, had to be unfixed and given the same elasticity as lines laid on transverse sleepers.

ABOVE Named after Jenny Lind, a Swedish singer popular with mid-nineteenth century British audiences, and designed in 1847 by David Joy, this neat 4-2-2 was built as a works venture by the Leeds Engine Foundry and sold to the London Brighton & South Coast Railway. Many were also exported.

LEFT Although intended to show the chaotic nature of the change-of-gauge at Gloucester, this engraving of 1853 in fact also shows how the railway companies provided elements to make it as efficient as possible: the platform at truck level and the derricks.

BELOW The curves and gradients of the Axminster–Lyme Regis branch of the LSWR led to to the retention of these 4-4-2 tank engines, designed by William Adams for the LSWR in 1882, into the 1960s.

BATTLE OF THE GAUGES

Despite some flirtations in East Anglia and Scotland with a 5ft (1.52m) or 5ft 6in (1.68m) gauge, the great majority of new schemes utilized the 4ft 8 ½in (1.43m) gauge established by George Stephenson. The only exceptions were schemes originated or supported by the Great Western, which insisted on Brunel's gauge being used. The

advantages and disadvantages of 'broad' or 'narrow' were widely argued. In 1844, Gloucester became the storm centre of the 'Battle of the Gauges'. Here the broad-gauge Bristol & Gloucester, allied to the Great Western, met the standard-gauge Birmingham & Gloucester. Every passenger and goods item travelling between Bristol and Birmingham had to be transferred to another train at Gloucester, with consequent delays. The GWR's proposed solution was to widen the track all the way to Birmingham, and talks on amalgamation were held in January 1845 with the Birmingham & Gloucester. Satisfactory financial terms were not reached, however, and the Midland Railway, in the person of its deputy chairman John Ellis, leapt into the gap. A deal was struck between the Midland and the two Gloucester companies, which resulted in the Midland leasing the lines of both and thus acquiring mainline access to Bristol. Not only was this a blow to the Great Western's expansion plans, it was a death blow to further development of the broad gauge.

At the end of 1844, broad-gauge mileage was just under 10 per cent of the total, then 2236 miles (3598km). But the broad gauge had the reputation of being faster, safer and more reliable. There were many railways still to be built, and the use of the narrower gauge did not seem inevitable. In one of its less hesitant forays into railway affairs, the government appointed a Gauge Commission in 1845. Despite acknowledging a far superior performance by broad-gauge engines, the Commissioners reported in early 1846 in favour of the narrower gauge. Parliament duly made it a requirement of all new railways to be of Stephenson's gauge, except when they were built as extensions to the broad-gauge lines already existing in the West Country, South Wales and the West Midlands.

ABOVE John Ramsbottom's 2-2-2 'Problem' class for the LNWR was a very successful type, despite its name. These locomotives were capable of hauling lightweight trains at high speed. During the 1860s, their regular duties were Liverpool and Manchester expresses and the Irish Mail. By now reduced to secondary services, No 803 *Tornado* stands at Carlisle in 1899.

2 · The Old Companies

Now part of the fabric of national life, the railway network spreads across the country in an ever more complex system, run by over a hundred companies. Often, they are competing for the same limited number of passengers, and the inevitable result is rivalry and hostility.

LEFT 'Flying Dutchman' was a famous racehorse of 1849, and the GWR named its morning mail train between London and Bristol as the *Dutchman*. Here, the down service passes Worle Junction behind a Gooch 4-2-2 on Brunel's original 'baulk road' track.

OPPOSITE A late Southern Railway style of lettering is shown on this South Eastern & Chatham P-class 0-6-0, designed under the charge of Harry Wainwright in 1910, built at Ashford Works, and originally intended for push-pull passenger service. The station is Tenterden, on the Kent & East Sussex Railway.

BETWEEN 1850 AND 1860, the pioneering and early phases came to an end. The railways were now part of national life and playing a vital role within the industrial and financial economy. By 1856, they were carrying double the amount of freight sent by canal. From its initial half-hearted efforts to exercise control, the government had backed off, and railway companies were in a state of free competition. The effects of this were more obvious in some areas than in others. Kent, with its commuter towns, farm traffic and lucrative cross-Channel routes, was served only by the South Eastern Railway until 1858. This monopoly was broken by the advent of the East Kent Railway (later renamed London Chatham & Dover). Every significant town in Kent, apart from Folkestone, was eventually served by both railways. The duplication was in most cases unnecessary and financially wasteful. The revenues were not great enough to make both companies profitable. As a result, the services offered by both were poor, the stations mean and the trains slow and dirty. The other side of competition was shown by the occasional flaring-up of price wars between the northern companies, which brought fares down for a short time at least.

The great men of the first generation had been the constructor-engineers. By the 1850s, with the trunk-route network largely established, the main railway companies had become large and complex businesses. The great men were now the general managers, such as Charles Saunders of the Great Western, John Ellis of the Midland and Edmund Denison of the Great Northern. Mostly these were men of vision and action, as well as of honesty, sagacity and common sense. Mostly, but not all. The first general manager of the London & North Western, Captain Mark Huish, has been described as 'perhaps the most ambitious figure which even Victorian industry can show'. Unlike George Hudson, Huish's pursuit of power was not motivated by money; he wanted power for its own sake. His ambitions were for the LNWR to dominate totally all other railways, and for himself to be the dictator of the LNWR. Seeing the independence and

BELOW Patrick Stirling designed this 4-2-2 class in 1870 for the Great Northern Railway, and No 1 has been preserved. Although considered by many to be one of the most beautiful of locomotives, and the favourite of Stirling himself, its outside cylinders and other visible means of traction were something of which he normally disapproved.

growing strength of the Great Northern as the main impediment to his goals, he set up an alliance known as the Euston Confederacy, drawing in the Midland, the Manchester Sheffield & Lincoln, the Lancashire & Yorkshire, and even the Eastern Counties and North British railways to hem in and obstruct the GNR.

UNSCRUPULOUS TACTICS

An ex-army man, Huish was combative and quarrelsome by nature. He was also a slippery negotiator whose word could not be trusted. Newspapers of the time called it 'the Battle of the Railways' when, in January 1856, the Great Northern and the London & North Western (the latter with its allies in the Confederacy) failed to renew an agreement on level-pegging fares and charges between London and towns in Yorkshire and Lincolnshire served by both lines. The Euston party were first to reduce fares. King's Cross followed suit, then Euston reduced the fares again, with further reductions following from the East Coast. Passenger traffic soared, but at no profit. 'If this goes on,' said Edmund Denison, chairman of the GN, 'I should think the great majority of my West Riding constituents, washed and unwashed, will visit London in the course of next week.' (Like several other railway chiefs, including Daniel Gooch and George Hudson, he was a member of Parliament.)

Something more akin to a war happened in 1850 on the less remunerative routes between Birkenhead and Birmingham, one operated by the Shrewsbury & Birmingham and Shrewsbury & Chester companies, the other by the Shropshire

ABOVE As suburban services became busier, longer trains and larger engines were needed. This imposing 4-6-4T was built by R.H. Whitelegg in 1922 for the Glasgow & South-Western Railway. The same designer had produced a very similar engine for the London Tilbury & Southend line in 1913. Unusually, the GSW engines could be driven from either side of the cab.

Union company, whose track was leased by the North Western. At the orders of Huish, the North Western applied illegal strong-arm tactics against the smaller companies and attempted to destroy their trade by charging ultra-low fares between Shrewsbury and Wolverhampton on his less direct route via Stafford. An army of North Western navvies forcibly prevented the Shrewsbury & Birmingham from getting a siding laid to the Birmingham Canal; troops had to be called out to halt the ensuing battle.

Huish then attempted to hijack the Shrewsbury & Birmingham by buying shares in it and passing them to his employees. In this way, a so-called shareholders' meeting illegally elected a new board of directors, who attempted to force through an alliance with the North Western. In the end, Huish was outmanoeuvred, and the Shrewsbury companies amalgamated with the Great Western, securing routes for the latter from London and South Wales to Birkenhead on Merseyside.

BELOW A publicity notice advertises the features offered by the East Coast Joint Service in the mid-1890s.

CORRIDOR LAVATORY CARRIAGES OF THE MOST IMPROVED DESCRIPTION ARE ATTACHED TO ALL THROUGH TRAINS. SLEEPING CARS ARE RUN ON ALL NIGHT TRAINS. CORRIDOR DINING CAR TRAINS RUN ON WEEK-DAYS BETWEEN EDINBURGH (WAVERLEY) AND LONDON (KING'S CROSS). FULL PARTICULARS OF TRAIN SERVICE ETC. CAN BE HAD ON APPLICATION TO THE SUPERINTENDENT. EAST COAST RAILWAYS, 32 WEST GEORGE STREET, GLASGOW.

By the later 1850s, time was running out for Captain Huish. His battles to increase the LNW empire had ultimately cost the company both profits and reputation. His frequent efforts to promote 'amalgamation' – for which read takeover – with the Great Western, the Midland and the Manchester Sheffield & Lincoln regularly came to nothing. He had broken agreements so often, and made so many enemies, that his confederacy fell apart. With heavy hints of his impending dismissal in the air, Huish submitted his resignation in September 1858 and disappeared from the railway scene.

OPPOSITE The invention of steam-powered sanding gear extended the life of the slippage-prone 'single driver'. Samuel Johnson's 4-2-2 'Spinner' class was built for the Midland Railway in 1900. It was the last and most powerful single, with some surviving into the 1920s. No 119, in immaculate condition, is seen here at Bedford in 1901.

THE BRITISH RAILWAY
SYSTEM IN 1852

IN SEARCH OF EASY MONEY

Far more of an out-and-out villain was John Parson, who presided over the affairs of the Oxford, Worcester & Wolverhampton Railway from 1851 to 1856. At least Huish was out to serve the interests of his company; Parson was one of those who saw the railway as a means of getting rich by chicanery. The OWW had been conceived as part of the Great Western's broad-gauge network, but its funds ran out before any building was done. Parson, failing to prise extra cash from the GWR, turned to its LNWR rivals and made a deal to build the line on standard gauge, though its enabling Act clearly specified broad gauge. For several years, Parson wriggled out of the Great Western's demands to have broad gauge laid. Largely to spite his rivals at Paddington, Huish sent his Euston–Wolverhampton trains via Bletchley to Oxford and thence over the OWW. Parson's only aim was to sell the company to the GWR – or anyone – for a handsome profit. In the end, the 'Old Worse and Worse' amalgamated with the Worcester & Hereford and Newport Abergavenny & Hereford railways, the combined line taking the name of West Midland Railway from 1860. In September 1861, the West Midland was

ABOVE Samuel Johnson's meticulous approach to design is shown in the symmetry of this Midland 2-4-0 Class 1 passenger engine.

OPPOSITE A diminutive 'Terrier' 0-6-0T, No 55, leaves Sheffield Park station on a Bluebell line train. This was class A1, designed by William Stroudley in 1872, for the London Brighton & South Coast Railway.

amalgamated with the Great Western. Parson was briefly a GW director and was last heard of when he resigned from the board of the Hammersmith & City line in London. Knowing that particular land would be required by the company, he had bought it at £820 an acre (0.4ha) and attempted to sell it to the company at £10,000 an acre.

The great majority of railway chairmen and officials, who were honest men, had also to be tough and suspicious-minded, as there were many people who saw railways as a way to easy money. Even under the eagle eye of Denison, the GNR was able to be swindled out of £220,000 between 1848 and 1856 by a relatively minor official, Leopold Redpath, head of the share registration department.

AUTOCRATS AT THE HELM

By training and custom, the men who ran the railways were autocrats. Sir Richard Moon, who ran the LNWR for 30 years from 1861, was the director chiefly responsible for speeding Huish on his way in 1858. He also fired the easy-going Francis Trevithick as chief mechanical engineer (CME) and replaced him with the far tougher John Ramsbottom. He terrified his directors as much as he did the staff. One very senior official, arriving one day at Euston at 9 a.m., was curtly informed: 'Sir, the North-Western starts work at eight.' Probably the greatest railway administrator of them all, Moon ran the company with iron rectitude. His officials were informed that 'a North-Western officer keeps his promises. But he will be careful what he promises in the first place'.

Some general managers were more open-minded than

ABOVE Former Southern Railway locomotives on shed at Reading in the mid-1950s: two Maunsell N-class fast goods 2-6-0s and one of the long-lived D1 4-4-0s.

BELOW The architecture of some country stations could at times verge on the sumptuous, as Chathill in Northumberland shows.

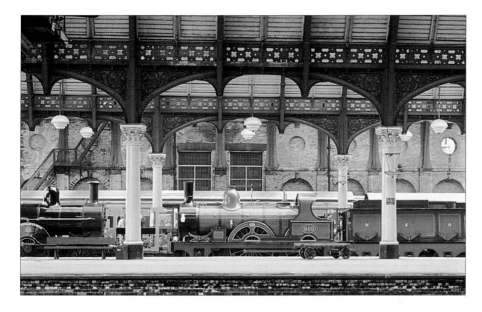

Conversation piece at York: framed by wrought-iron columns and girders, two preserved veteran engines rest at the platform in a scene that replicates the steam age of the 1890s.

others, and progress often tended to come from those who had experience of other systems than the British. James Allport, who had begun as one of Hudson's lieutenants, went to the USA before returning and ultimately taking charge of the Midland Railway. Apart from astute if sometimes devious management to enlarge his company – which he extended from central England to become the third Anglo-Scottish main line – he studied the tastes and needs of all its customers, actual and potential. In 1872, the Midland put third-class carriages on all of its trains. Other lines continued with first and second only, third still being relegated to the Parliamentary train or to inconvenient hours. Two years later, Allport went further and abolished second class – in effect turning third into second by replacing the wooden seats with cushions. Other companies were outraged at such pandering to the public, but all had to follow the Midland's lead (some took a very long time). At the top end of the price scale, Allport was also responsible for introducing Pullman cars from the USA to Great Britain. They did not form whole trains, but were attached to the Anglo-Scottish expresses.

BELOW In the heart of the Grampians, at the highest point reached by British mainline railways (1484ft/ 452m), a Jones 'Big Goods' 4-6-0 of the Highland Railway shows it has steam to spare as it hauls a Perth–Inverness goods through the Pass of Drumochter.

Another managerial figure with a visionary streak was Sir Edward Watkin, who trained in the school of Huish, but ended as a baronet and elder statesman. Watkin was the planner of the new Great Central route from the Midlands to London, but long before that his grand scheme was a Channel tunnel, which would be the Paris branch of his South Eastern and Manchester Sheffield & Lincoln companies (he was also chairman of the Metropolitan Railway). Preliminary diggings were made in 1871, but the plan was stopped by opposition from the War Office (still with a Napoleonic Wars mentality), prompted, it was alleged, by James Staats Forbes, wily chairman of the London Chatham & Dover, who did not want to lose his lucrative boat-train traffic. Also, Watkin was chairman of the South Eastern, and both companies, from the chairmen down, were at war with each other over the Kentish and Continental traffic.

Under the chairman or general manager was a hierarchy of senior officers. The locomotive superintendent was one, but it was now managers rather than engineers who

LEFT The Midland Railway's monogram in tilework, from the station at Shackerstone, Leicestershire. Although the era of brands was yet to come, all the railway companies set great store by public recognition. Conscious of being among the country's biggest businesses, they were proud of their identity.

BELOW The few controls and spartan layout of the enginemen's cab are seen in this unusual shot of the Great Northern Railway's 4-2-2 No 1, waiting in line outside King's Cross Station to be attached to its train. The driver is on the right.

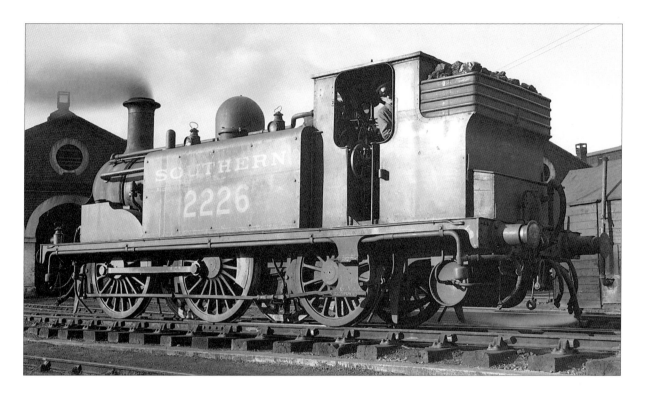

ran the business. The traffic manager, who was responsible for timetabling, providing services and charges, was perhaps the key official. The locomotive department was there to provide the necessary power, at carefully controlled cost. There was still ample room for invention and development in railway matters. John Ramsbottom, chief mechanical engineer of the LNWR, laid the first-ever locomotive water troughs at Mochdre, on the Chester–Holyhead line, in 1860. The choice of this line was no whim. Over it ran the Irish Mail, at this time the only fast train on the LNWR. The lucrative Post Office mail contract specified tight timing, and the company had no intention of losing the contract. A gifted engineer, Ramsbottom also devised a new and much improved safety valve, although he is chiefly remembered for his reorganization of Crewe Works into a highly efficient factory, which was a true predecessor of the twentieth-century production line.

0-4-2 DI TANK LBSCR 1873

Tractive effort: 12,500lb (5,670kg)

Axle load: 30,240lb (13.7 tonnes)

Cylinders: two 17x24in (416x609mm)

Driving wheels: 66in (167cm)

Heating surface: 1020sq ft (94.75m²)

Superheater: n/a

Steam pressure: 140psi (9.9kg/cm²)

Grate area: 15sq ft (1.4m²)

Fuel: Coal – 1120lb (0.5 tonne)

Water: 860gall (1037 US) (3.9m³)

Total weight: 86,240lb (39.1 tonnes)

Overall length: 15ft (4.57m)

TIMELY CHANGES

As the steam railway spread across the country, it introduced for the first time a national standard of time. For centuries, country towns had set their own clocks without a care as to what time it was elsewhere. Now, with the introduction of timetables and a requirement to maintain punctuality, time became important and stations had to conform. The process was aided by the use of the electric telegraph. The lineside poles and wires became a familiar feature of the steam railway. Later, the telephone became a vital instrument. At one time, indeed, it seemed that the railway stations might act as telegraph offices for the towns they served, but the monopoly on telecommunications was eventually given to the Post Office. The process of standardizing time

ABOVE William Stroudley's D1 0-4-2T first appeared in 1875, and it was a highly successful and long-lived class. This one, No 2226 of the Southern Railway, was at Stewarts Lane depot in 1936.

was slow and uneven, and it was not until 1880 that Greenwich Mean Time became the official and legal standard throughout Great Britain. Among the innumerable side effects of the railway was a boom in the clock-making business.

Even when times were standardized, commercial hostility and the resultant lack of liaison meant that railway companies were slow to provide the benefits of a system of interconnections. Traffic managers preferred to seek running powers over neighbouring lines in order to convey passengers in their own trains all the way. At this period, it would also have been very difficult to achieve the necessary precision of timing. But some companies, such as the Great North of Scotland, became notorious for deliberately obstructing the possibility of connections. Their northbound trains were despatched from their Aberdeen terminus even if there were passengers from the Caledonian station were hammering on the gate.

One aspect of railway operation which left much to be desired throughout the 1860s and 1870s was that of safety. Crucial to safe travel were three things: effective signalling, block working and automatic braking. The lack of the first two of these was brought home by the Clayton Tunnel crash on the LBSCR on 25 August 1861. Trains were still despatched on the time-interval system: when a stationmaster judged that enough time had elapsed since the previous train's departure, he let the next one go. Signals, where in use, were often unreliable. The signal controlling access to the Clayton Tunnel was worked by the train, turning to 'danger' as the train went by. On this occasion, however, it failed to do so. Alerted by the signalman, who had noticed this, the driver of the next train came to a stop in the tunnel. A third train, despatched from Brighton after too short an interval, also passed the defective signal as well as the signalman and ran into the stationary train, causing 11 deaths.

OPPOSITE The first British 4-6-0, No 103 of the Highland Railway, built in 1894 and now preserved, is seen on a special mixed-train run on the Dingwall–Skye line, skirting Loch Carron between Plockton and Strome Ferry, with the Skye Cuillin in the background.

BELOW When continental travel was for the privileged few: the London Chatham & Dover's paddle steamer *Maid of Kent*, launched in 1861, meets the waiting LC&D boat train, with four 4-wheel carriages, at the Admiralty Pier, Dover, some time during the 1860s.

STEP BY STEP TO SAFETY

The ensuing Board of Trade enquiry pressed for the imposition of block working. This, of course, required a fully signalled line, so that trains could maintain one 'block' of track free between them. Not unaware of the cost of this, the railway companies preferred to put the onus on the engine crew to keep a lookout ahead. In its defence, the Brighton company pointed out that reliance on mechanical aids was a main cause of the Clayton smash.

In 1856, the first interlocking frame, combining points and signals, was installed at the busy Bricklayer's Arms junction in South London. A fully interlocking frame was set up at Kentish Town, North London, in 1860. The signals could not show a clear road unless the points were correctly set. Single-line working was governed by clear rules; however, when these were ignored, nasty accidents could happen. One was at Thorpe, Norwich, on the GER on 10 September 1874, when up and down expresses were allowed to collide on a single-line section. By this time, block working was practised on about half the main lines of the country. But many lines were wholly or partly single-tracked, and it was not until 1878, when Edward Tyer patented the electric tablet instrument, which allowed access to a particular stretch of line to only one train

BELOW Locomotives might suffer misadventures, but usually could be repaired. This Southern C2x class 0-6-0, designed by R.B. Billinton for the London Brighton & South Coast Railway, fell into a stream bed while hauling a local goods near Midhurst in November 1951, but was back on the rails in 1952.

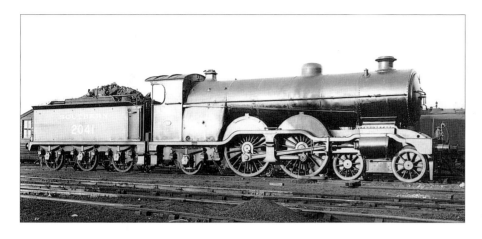

LEFT An example of the handsome H-class Atlantics designed by D. Earle Marsh for the London Brighton & South Coast Railway between 1905 and 1911. He was an ex-GNR man, and his locomotives have a distinct Doncaster look.

at a time, that single-line working became – almost – foolproof. A chapter of minor errors led to a head-on collision on the single-track Cambrian line between Abermule and Newtown, in January 1921, causing 17 deaths.

The third essential, an automatic braking system, was unknown on British railways in the 1860s. Most trains relied on a combination of the engine's brakes and a hand-operated brake in the guard's van. Continuous brakes throughout the train were rare. Some lines, including the LNWR and the North London Railway, used chain brakes, operated from the brake van on two or three other brake vans fitted into a long train, but most lines had none at all. On 23 August 1858, 17 people were killed in a smash on the Oxford, Worcester & Wolverhampton Railway, when a train comprising 30 carriages parted and 18 ran backwards downhill to collide with a following train.

Little progress on braking was made over the next 15 years until, following a number of bad accidents, a Royal Commission on Railway Accidents was set up in 1875; in June of that year the Midland organized a series of brake trials on its Nottingham–Newark branch. Several companies sent trains, fitted with different systems. The most

BELOW GWR 'Castle' class 4-6-0 No 5032 *Usk Castle* emerges from the Severn Tunnel, Britain's longest at 4 miles 628 yds (7km), with a South Wales–Paddington express. The crew are at pains to minimize smoke output, despite the adverse gradient as the line rises to ground level.

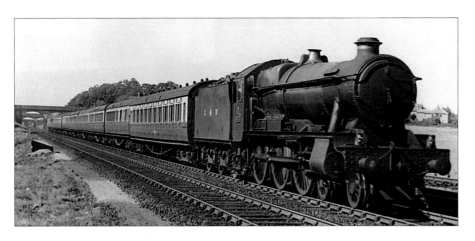

LEFT GWR 4-6-0 1027, of the post-war 'County' class. A powerful mixed-traffic type, this engine is from the 1947 production batch and was built, like the great majority of GWR locomotives, at Swindon. A double chimney was provided for all the 'Counties' in 1955.

effective was the American Westinghouse automatic air brake, favoured by the Midland itself. Another American system, Smith's non-automatic vacuum brake, was taken up by some companies, including the Manchester Sheffield & Lincolnshire. Its fatal disadvantage was that if the train parted in two, the brake immediately became ineffective. A crash at Penistone on the MSL on 16 July 1884 demonstrated this at the cost of 24 lives. It was only in 1889, following a serious accident at Armagh in Ireland, that government action compelled the companies to install effective continuous automatic brakes on passenger trains. Although the technology had been available for nearly 15 years, little had been done. Reluctance to spend money on installing efficient

BELOW The preserved GWR 'City'-class 4-4-0 *City of Truro* was the first British locomotive to be recorded as exceeding 100mph (160km/h) on 9 May 1904, on an 'Ocean Mail' special descending Wellington Bank between Plymouth and Bristol.

systems and perhaps a xenophobic dislike of American technology were the only hold-ups. It was a discreditable episode.

DECLINING APPEAL

During the 1860s to 1880s generally, the railways did not enjoy great public esteem. Safety concerns were only one reason for this. The economic depression of the mid-century had reduced business expansion, and many companies were short of money. Apart from a few lines, such as the coal-carrying Taff Vale, the railways themselves were not in any case as profitable as had once been hoped: this was partly because they

ABOVE This slightly ungainly-looking 4-4-2, *President*, represents G.J. Churchward's close interest in the work of Alfred De Glehn, of the Nord railway in France, while working on the design of his first 4-6-0s in 1903. Above the waist it looks impeccably Great Western; below, it is a French four-cylinder compound.

LEFT Filling tenders with coal was a necessary task in preparing a locomotive for service. This hopper-and-chute method, from a raised coaling track, helped to speed up the process. The engine is GWR 4-4-0 3702 *Halifax*, a 'City' class rebuilt from the 'Atbara' class in 1908.

ran so many duplicated or loss-making services, started up to fend off or challenge a rival company. Investors were not seeing a very good return for their money.

Rail travel was a spartan affair, especially in cold weather. Most carriages were still uncomfortable and unheated. Although experiments were being made with gas lighting, most carriages were lit by sooty oil-burning pot-lamps. Foot warmers were available for first-class passengers only. Corridor stock with toilets was a rare luxury, even in first. Some very old rolling-stock was still in use. Trains were usually very slow. This was partly because of the deficient brakes and absence of signals; partly because the permanent way was often unable to cope with high speeds; and not least because going faster was more expensive for the railway company. The travelling public had long ago became used to the novelty of rail travel; what they wanted now was a safe and comfortable service. The public could also see that many railway services were unnecessarily slow, and the entrenched hostility among the companies irritated most people.

Railway managements were often chiefly inspired by the need to economize, led in this respect by Sir Richard Moon on the Premier Line. 'It is so much easier to get over a difficulty by increasing the quantity by a large outlay of money than to arrange for properly using what we have got,' wrote Moon in a memorandum on the subject of tarpaulin covers for goods wagons. No item was too small for him to take account of.

The heroic age was past, it seemed. Yet one or two undertakings on a heroic scale were still to be noted. One was the Severn Tunnel, opened for goods traffic in September 1886 after 14 years of struggle against underground springs and seawater incursions. Daniel Gooch, who had left the Great Western in 1864 and was invited

OPPOSITE TOP Divers at work in late December 1879 at the site of the Tay Bridge collapse. The engine that fell, North British Railway 4-4-0 No 229, was hoisted up, repaired and ran for many years. It was known to staff as 'The Diver', and no driver would take it over the new Tay Bridge.

OPPOSITE BOTTOM The opulence of first class: a padded door leads into a thickly carpeted compartment with panelled wood interior in this preserved six-wheeled carriage of the South Eastern & Chatham Railway.

LEFT The massive scale of the Forth Bridge (opened in 1890) is captured in this shot of an LNER A4 Pacific passing through the girders of one of the three great cantilever sections.

back to become its chairman in 1866, was the first man through when the headings met on 27 October 1884. At 4 miles 682 yards (7.06km), it was the longest railway tunnel in the country.

Then there was the Tay Bridge. North of Edinburgh, the wide firths of Forth and Tay compelled all northbound rail traffic to go round via Stirling and Perth. The world's first train ferry, *Leviathan*, was put in service across the Firth of Forth, for goods wagons and deck passengers only, in February 1850. A similar craft was built for the Firth of Tay. Their designer was a versatile engineer, Thomas Bouch, who had also designed the high iron viaducts on the Stockton & Darlington line between Darlington and Kirkby Stephen. When the decision was taken to bridge the easier Firth of Tay in 1870, it was Bouch to whom John Stirling of Kippendavie, the North British chairman, turned. In 1873, Bouch was also appointed as engineer of a bridge to be built over the Firth of Forth. The single-track Tay Bridge, longest in the world at 3884yds (4247m) was passed for service in February 1878, and on 20 June Queen Victoria crossed it on the way from Balmoral to Windsor. On the evening of 28 December 1879, the bridge collapsed in a gale, taking with it a train. About 80 people were killed. The subsequent enquiry found the bridge to have been incompetently designed, built and maintained. Bouch succumbed to death soon afterwards, and his design for a great suspension bridge over the Forth was consigned to oblivion.

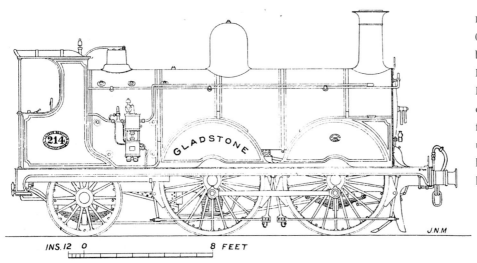

INS.12 0   8 FEET

LEFT William Stroudley's 0-4-2 'Gladstone' type was built for the London Brighton & South Coast Railway from 1885. Its lack of truck or bogie wheels in front of the drivers was unusual in a fast passenger locomotive, but it proved highly successful in service.

BRIDGE AND REPUTATION REBUILT

Kippendavie nevertheless pressed on to have the Tay Bridge rebuilt, and a new design was commissioned for the Forth Bridge. This time there were no corners cut. The new double-track Tay Bridge was opened on 13 June 1887. Then, 4 March 1890 saw the opening of the Forth Bridge, with its triple cantilever towers the mightiest monument to Victorian engineering, completing the direct East Coast route between London and Aberdeen. As such a structure was beyond the resources of the North British Railway alone, the Forth Bridge Railway was a joint venture of all the East Coast companies.

The railway companies had battled for their independence from government control, if not entirely from regulation. In the process, they perhaps invented the PR man, in the person of Sir Henry Cole, who was retained by the London & North Western in 1846 to 'create a public opinion' against the broad gauge. But they could not entirely be laws unto themselves. Competition with rivals – and, increasingly, the power of public opinion – had to be taken into account. Public opinion went all the way up to Queen Victoria, who had strong views on railways, chiefly to do with speed (the pace of the Royal train was always a decorous one).

BELOW Originally built in 1879 as a 2-2-2T, this Highland Railway tank engine was rebuilt by David Jones as a 4-4-0T and served as a shunter at Inverness into the 1940s. Its front end design perpetuates the Allan 'Crewe' type, although the louvred chimney was a Jones speciality.

0-4-2 GLADSTONE LBSCR 1882

Tractive effort: 13,200lb (5986kg)
Axle load: 32,480lb (14.7 tonnes)
Cylinders: two 18¼x26in (463x660mm)
Driving wheels: 78in (198cm)
Heating surface: 1485.4sq ft (138m²)
Superheater: n/a
Steam pressure: 140psi (9.9kg/cm²)
Grate area: 20.65sq ft (1.9m²)
Fuel: Coal – 8960lb (4 tonnes)
Water: 3000gall (3603 US) (13.6m³)
Total weight: 86,800lb (39.3 tonnes)
Overall length: 15ft 7in (4.75m)

In the early years, the companies had treated passengers with a degree of suspicion and disdain: suspicion because they might injure themselves and demand compensation (this was based on the income of the sufferer, to the alarm of the Great Northern when a bishop and the Lord Mayor of London were involved in a collision in 1853); disdain because the companies felt they had a safe monopoly, and, anyway, passengers got in the way of efficient working. Late in the century, the Great North of Scotland Railway (which enjoyed a monopoly in its area) would still unlock the compartment doors one by one at Aberdeen, ensuring that each was full before the next was opened. More typical was Edmund Denison, exhorting his staff in 1850: 'Formerly when the London & Birmingham and the Midland lines were opened, people were almost obliged to go down on their knees to be allowed to enter a carriage. Now directors and managers have to make a most civil and respectful bow to parties to coax them to go.' The campaign for good manners on the Great Northern brought it more custom at a time when the North Western tolerated or encouraged the old arrogance. Even so, passengers were often victims of intercompany feuds.

ABOVE 'Gladstone' 0-4-2 *Allen Sarle* at Oxted, LBSCR, 1901. Like all Stroudley's engines, it is painted in his very bright 'Improved Engine Green'. Behind the tender is a fine example of a ducketed brake van, the extended windows of which allowed the guard a fore-and-aft view of the train.

REGIONAL DOMINANCE

In 1860, although there were by now more than a hundred companies, the pattern of regional dominance was clear. In the South, the territories radiated from London. The

London Chatham & Dover and the South Eastern were still locked in a somewhat sluggish battle for Kent. The London Brighton & South Coast served the towns of Sussex. The London & South Western ran through Surrey, dividing into main lines to Southampton and west to Basingstoke, Salisbury and Exeter. The Great Western's narrow corridor from Paddington opened out into the broad fan of Wessex, Devon and Wales. Most of it was still broad gauge, although some frontier lines were mixed gauge. The London & North Western ran to the Midlands and beyond to Liverpool and Manchester. The Great Northern's domain stretched up to York, extending east and west between Sheffield and Lincoln. The Great Eastern ran north-east to Colchester, Ipswich and Norwich. Further north, the map includes the great enclave of the Midland around Nottingham, Leicester, Derby and Birmingham. Further still, the Lancashire & Yorkshire spread across the Pennines between those two counties. The North Eastern controlled most of the lines north of York. Beyond the border, two large companies, the Caledonian and the North British, controlled most Scottish lines, apart from the south-west corner, occupied by the Glasgow & South Western Railway.

It was not a static picture, however. The biggest, and still growing, industrial cities – Manchester, Birmingham, Leeds, Sheffield – were magnets to all companies with a hope of reaching them, whether by building a new line or by obtaining running powers on an existing railway. Intertwined with the LNWR, Midland and GNR, the Manchester Sheffield & Lincoln, managed with suave aggressiveness by Edward Watkin, survived by constantly playing off one of the larger companies against the others. Many small companies owned some of the lines used by the giants: in due course they would be absorbed by one or another. The proprietors of the short Trent Valley Railway, which provided a bypass to the east side of Birmingham, through Lichfield, did extremely well out of its sale to the LNWR in 1845.

Other small companies managed to preserve their independence. Some, such as the North Staffordshire, did so by a kind of symbiosis with a mighty neighbour, in this case the North Western. Other running systems wriggled across several of the giants' preserves, but with routes no one was in a hurry to snatch. These usually ended up as jointly owned. Among them were the Midland and Great Northern Joint, a collection of local East Anglian lines embracing King's Lynn and Norwich, with later outliers to

ABOVE Excursion and special traffic was a lucrative extra revenue-earner for the railways, utilizing plant at weekends and holiday times. The Great Northern was a leader in this sort of traffic.

BELOW It was Samuel Johnson who developed the deep crimson lake colour which distinguished Midland, and later LMS, express engines from 1873 until 1939. Here, it is set off to great effect by the polished brasswork of this 4-2-2, a 7ft 6in (2.28m) bogie single of 1889.

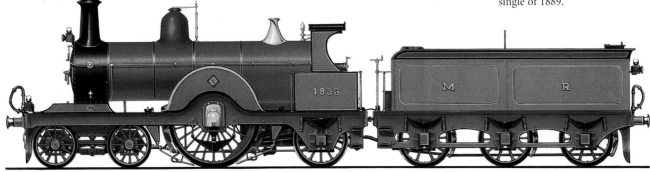

Yarmouth and Cromer. They formed the Eastern & Midlands Railway in 1882 and were bought up jointly by the Midland and the Great Northern in 1893. Its headquarters remained at King's Lynn, and it had its own works at Melton Constable, maintaining and sometimes building its own yellow-liveried engines. In Wessex, there was the Somerset & Dorset, jointly run by the Midland and the South Western, cutting right across Great Western territory between Bath and Bournemouth with distinctive blue-painted engines. In the North West was the largest and busiest joint operation, the Cheshire Lines Committee, with a network of lines between Chester and Manchester. Formed in 1867 by a partnership between the Midland, the Manchester

ABOVE A Great Western broad-gauge train travelling on dual-gauge track. The engine is scarcely wider than the track (compare page 149). If the GWR had taken full advantage of the potential of the broad gauge, British locomotives may have dwarfed even those of Russia.

LEFT GWR 'Duke'-class 4-4-0 *Comet* at Swindon: Swindon's 4-4-0s had a look very much of their own, with outside axle-boxes on the bogie wheels, inside cylinders and cranks set outside the frames.

LEFT With cranks flying around outside the frame, a GWR 'Bulldog' 4-4-0, No 3410 *Columbia*, speeds a semi-fast train from Birmingham Snow Hill to Worcester and Hereford, along the former 'Old Worse and Worse' line, in 1934.

OPPOSITE The west side of Waverley Station, Edinburgh, in the 1950s. The station pilot, an ex-North British J83 0-6-0T, draws out a train of empty stock, while a Gresley Pacific waits for the off with a northbound express. The North British station hotel looms above the platforms.

Sheffield & Lincoln and the Great Northern, it used its owners' engines, but had its own carriages and wagons, and continued to do so until November 1948.

A small independent survivor was the Midland & South Western Junction, tracing a path through the Cotswolds and the Downs from Andoversford, near Cheltenham, to Andover on the South Western main line to Salisbury. In 1891, the year of its inception, it went into receivership, but the man put in by the receivers to run the line, Sam Fay, re-energized the company, made it pay and set up exemplary cross-country connections from Southampton (LSWR) to points as remote as Bradford and Liverpool. Few managers had the drive and ability of Fay, who later became general manager of the very much larger LSWR and ultimately of the Great Central.

FILLING THE GAPS

Although the building of new railways continued right through the nineteenth century and into the twentieth, it was largely a matter of filling gaps (real or imagined) and, in several cases, shortening city-to-city routes – as with the Midland's Chinley cut-off via the long Totley Tunnel between Manchester and Sheffield, completed in 1893; the Great Western cut-offs, of which the most notable were the South Wales & Bristol Direct, bypassing Bristol to the north; and the Castle Cary–Langport line, completing an alternative main line

BELOW The Midland Railway coat of arms was proudly displayed in stations and on the side of every locomotive.

2-4-2T L&YR 1889

Tractive effort: 16,900lb (7,664kg)
Axle load: 35,448lb (16 tonnes)
Cylinders: two (i) 18x26in (457x660mm)
Driving wheels: 67 ¾in (172cm)
Heating surface: 1,216.4sq ft (113m²)
Superheater: n/a
Steam pressure: 160psi (11.3kg/cm²)
Grate area: 18.75sq ft (1.7m²)
Fuel: Coal – 5,600lb (2.5 tonnes)
Water: 1,340gall (1,609 US) (6m³)
Total weight: 125,328lb (56.8 tonnes)
Overall length: 24ft 4in (7.42m)

between Reading and Taunton and at last enabling the GWR, long sneered at as the 'Great Way Round', to rival the timings of London–Exeter trains via Salisbury on the LSWR. Both of these were completed early in the twentieth century.

In remoter parts of the country, however, several major lines had not been built by 1860. In the central Highlands, the Perth & Dunkeld line was linked in 1864 to the Inverness & Aberdeen at Forres by a long railway rising to 1484ft (452m) in the Druimuachdar Pass, the highest point to be reached by a British mainline railway. In 1865, this, as the Inverness & Perth Junction, became part of the newly formed Highland Railway, with its headquarters and works at Inverness. The Highland gradually extended itself north to Thurso, on the Pentland Firth, although the mainline terminus was Wick, reached in 1874. At the same time, the Callander & Oban extension of the Caledonian was being built, although Oban was not finally reached until 1880.

The 1860s also saw railway development in central Wales, with the Oswestry & Newtown Railway, open by 1861, linking up with the already built but isolated Llanidloes & Newtown. By early 1863, the Newtown & Machynlleth was open. Aberystwyth was reached in 1865, and the northward line via the Mawddach Viaduct to Pwllheli was completed in October 1867. In the far South-West of England, the LSWR had endured somewhat restricted access to Plymouth from its Lydford branch

ABOVE Placed in service in 1889, and now preserved, L&Y No. 1008 was the first locomotive to be built at the new Horwich Works, and leader of a very numerous class. It has radial axles at each end and water pick-up apparatus for running both forward and backward.

OPPOSITE Richard Maunsell's South Eastern & Chatham Railway L-class 4-4-0s were known as 'Germans', as the first 11 of the type were built by Borsig of Berlin in 1914. Still on mainline service in the 1950s, the L and its development, the L1, were often 'clocked' by enthusiasts at speeds of more than 70mph (112km/h).

The Cambrian Railway's viaduct across the Mawddach at Barmouth, built in 1867, is the longest wooden structure of its kind in Britain. At the northern end, a metal bowstring-girder section was built as a swing bridge to enable coastal vessels to sail up the estuary. A Shrewsbury–Pwllheli train is crossing.

by way of the GWR Yelverton branch. In 1890, it leased the new Plymouth Devonport & South-Western Junction Railway, down the Tamar Valley to its own station at Plymouth Friary. With its London–Salisbury–Exeter main line, opened in July 1860, the LSWR picked off the South Devon seaside towns east of the Exe. By careful and delicate stages, it extended itself through North Devon and into Cornwall by what appeared to be a succession of branch lines, but which by 1899, when it reached its

westernmost point at Padstow, made a sort of main line for holiday traffic (the proudly named Atlantic Coast Express would operate from 1926), as well as for a respectable amount of fish traffic.

To Carlisle in Comfort

Some of these lines would be barely profitable, but their social value in opening up remote or mountain country was indisputable. The need for the Midland Railway to construct a new main line from the West Riding of Yorkshire to Carlisle was less obvious, especially to the LNWR, which, with the Caledonian, had enjoyed a monopoly on the West Coast route to Glasgow from the very beginning. Since 1858, the Midland had found a way into London by agreeing running powers with the Great Northern from Hitchin into King's Cross. The GN line was heavily congested, and, by the early 1860s, the Midland was building its own line south from Bedford towards a new terminus at St Pancras.

The thought of a London–Scotland Midland service was immensely appealing to a number of companies. At Carlisle, two potential allies eagerly awaited the Midland traffic: the Glasgow & South-Western Railway, with its line to Glasgow via Dumfries, and the NBR with its new (1862) Border Union line linking Edinburgh and Carlisle via Hawick. A further ally was the Lancashire & Yorkshire, which was also irked by the LNWR monopoly. When at one point the Midland lost confidence and sought to

BELOW On a Bristol– Birmingham service in 1921, Midland 4-4-0 No 525, a rebuild by R.M. Deeley of Johnson's '60' class (1898), breasts the Lickey Incline at Blackwell, with a banking engine at the rear of the train. The station equipment, including the oil lamp, is of interest.

abandon the project, the L&Y and the Scottish companies forced it back on the rails. Rising to 1151ft (351m) at Ais Gill summit, the line had heavy engineering works, including two long tunnels and the Ribblehead Viaduct, and, although it received Parliamentary assent in 1866, it was not finished until 1875, when freight traffic began. Passenger traffic began on 1 May 1876, with sumptuous new Pullman car expresses which outdid all rivals for comfort. The new line became well patronized, and its arrival added to the excitements of Carlisle Citadel Station, a frontier point where the expresses changed engines, the shiny black of the LNWR replaced by the royal blue of the CR, or Midland red by the varying greens of its two Scottish allies. In addition to these, the local Maryport & Carlisle and the North Eastern (coming in from Newcastle) companies also used the station.

ABOVE D. Earle Marsh's express class I3 4-4-2T of the London Brighton & South Coast Railway, a type which astonished the engineers of the LNWR in 1909 by its frugal consumption of coal and water, when tested against their own 2-4-0 'Precedent' *Titan* between Rugby and Brighton.

Especially from the 1870s to around 1914, the great interchange stations, such as Carlisle, York, Perth and Chester, were colourful, bustling places. The variety of different engine types and company liveries caught the eye. The walls were covered with advertisement placards for a great diversity of products. There was much impressive activity. Portions of the train were detached or added. Engines were changed or watered. All sorts of things in the way of goods and luggage were seen on the platforms. The railways had an obligation as 'common carrier' to transport all manner of items. It was not unusual to see an entire circus, or the stock and equipment of a farm, being trundled slowly through by one of the ubiquitous 0-6-0 types that formed close on half the locomotive stock. The station was usually open to the public, and tickets were checked at a ticket platform outside the main station. A large and varied staff was employed, from the wheel-tapper with his hammer to the boy selling sweets from a tray; from the stationmaster himself to the lamplighter who topped up and lit the oil lamps inside the carriages before dusk. Beyond the knowledge of the passenger, each

LEFT To the annoyance of company accountants, turntables had to be regularly rebuilt and extended towards the end of the nineteenth century, as engines became longer. This Crewe-type 2-4-0 of the E&MR (later Midland & Great Northern Joint) fits comfortably for the time being.

company had its own facilities close to these 'joint' stations: engine shed, carriage sidings and goods yard. More small engines fussed about on transfer trips between the yards. Officials of the Railway Clearing House monitored all intercompany movements and reported back to the (by now) huge head office by Euston Station.

MORE POWER NEEDED

Trains were longer and heavier than in the early period, especially after the mid-1870s, when all companies followed Midland practice – with different degrees of effectiveness – in improving passenger comfort. The consequences for railway accountants were important, as fewer passengers per ton of train pushed up operating costs. The consequences for locomotive design were also important.

ABOVE The preserved GNR single-driver, No 1, in 1982. The engine, once used for hauling mainline expresses between London and York, remains in working order.

2-4-0 PRECEDENT LNWR 1874	
Tractive effort:	10,400lb (4716kg)
Axle load:	25,760lb (11.7 tonnes)
Cylinders:	two 17x24in (432x609mm)
Driving wheels:	79½in (202cm)
Heating surface:	1083sq ft (100.5m²)
Superheater:	n/a
Steam pressure:	140psi (9.9kg/cm²)
Grate area:	17.1sq ft (1.6 m²)
Fuel:	Coal – 8960lb (4 tonnes)
Water:	1800gall (2162 US) (8.2m³)
Total weight:	86,128lb (39 tonnes)
Overall length:	18ft 1in (5.51m)

Unless trains were to be expensively double-headed, more powerful engines were essential. In the last decades of the nineteenth century, an extraordinary variety of locomotive types existed. But, livery and incidental details aside, they were mostly variations on a limited number of well-established themes.

There was still a clear distinction between goods and passenger engines. The goods engines at this time were slightly larger versions of the old 2-4-0 and 0-6-0 types, otherwise little changed. Heavy trains, such as the Midland and GN coal trains to London,

LEFT Francis Webb's LNWR 2-4-0s were officially known as the 'Precedents', after the first engine in the class; however, to enginemen and enthusiasts, they were better known as 'Jumbos'. Here, No 5048 *Henry Pease* takes on coal. Some of the 'Jumbos' remained in service for more than 50 years.

were usually hauled by two engines. Just around the turn of the nineteenth century, a notable feature, caused by production bottlenecks in British locomotive works, was the arrival of 2-6-0 mixed-traffic engines, imported from the USA by several companies, including the Midland, Great Northern and Great Central. Importation of foreign types was always rare, and such an influx was unusual. Their appearance was heavily anglicized, but the Midland examples did have generous American-style cabs. Although passenger engines frequently hauled goods trains, and vice versa, these were the first tender engines in Britain to occupy this in-between status.

Until the Midland's revolutionary developments of the 1870s, passenger engines were built to haul lightweight trains at a fair speed. Unlike the practice on European railways, most British lines operated frequent but short trains. This resulted in the continuation of the single-driver passenger engine, with its one pair of very large-diameter driving wheels. The most impressive of these were the Great Western's, built for the broad gauge by Gooch's engineering successors, Joseph Armstrong and William Dean; the most famous were the elegant Great Northern singles designed by Patrick Stirling. That designer's own favourite, his 'grand engine', was the bogie 4-2-2 of 1870, with driving wheels 96in (244cm) in diameter and – unexpectedly – outside cylinders (the height of the driving axle made inside cylinders impossible). Somewhat to the

ABOVE Southern D-class 4-4-0 as BR 31746, photographed on a local train at St Catherine's, Guildford, in 1951. The D class, designed by Robert Surtees for the South Eastern & Chatham Railway in 1900, was a most reliable engine, and numerous examples survived virtually unaltered for over 50 years.

LEFT The Caledonian Railway's one-off bogie 'single' No 123, with 7ft (2.13m) driving wheels, built by Neilson & Co of Glasgow in 1886 and shown at the Edinburgh Exhibition of that year, was a participant in the 1888 'Race to the North'. Reboilered in 1905, it was retired in 1935 after running 780,000 miles (1,255,288km) and is the only preserved Caledonian express engine.

surprise of American and European visitors, such engines worked mainline expresses into the twentieth century, and at high speed.

The 2-4-0 was also widely used in passenger service. Some hard-slogging but simple and robust engines of this type lasted a very long time: a Kirtley 2-4-0 of 1866, No 158 of the Midland Railway, was still running on the LMS 77 years later as No 20002. Perhaps the most famous examples of the type were Francis Webb's LNWR 'Precedent' class, popularly known as 'Jumbos'. One of these, *Charles Dickens*, clocked up more than two million miles of running, all on the Manchester–Euston service, between 1882 and 1902. But heavy trains, with dining cars, sleepers or Pullmans, required more adhesive weight on the rails than the 4-2-2 or 2-4-0 could provide. As a result, from 1870 to 1899, the 4-4-0 engine dominated passenger traffic.

AMERICAN INFLUENCE

Although the classic British 4-4-0 is thought of as having inside frames and cylinders and a low running-plate, with half of each wheel hidden by a splasher, this was not the first version of that wheel arrangement to run. The bogie, a four-wheeled frame provided with a degree of independent movement, was developed in the USA and taken up in Britain from the 1850s; apart from spreading the weight of the front end, it was supposed to guide the engine into sharp curves. Many designers were wary of it and never used it; its earliest designs were never quite satisfactory, and it continued to exercise designers right up to the 1930s.

A satisfactory bogie was, however, developed by Robert Stephenson & Co and first used in 1865 by William Adams on 4-4-0T engines for the North London Railway. British workshops built bogie 4-4-0s for export for several years before any were used by home companies. In 1860, the Stockton & Darlington bought from Robert Stephenson & Co a pair of outside-cylinder, inside-framed 4-4-0s for its trans-Pennine service to Penrith, the first tender type of this wheel arrangement for home service, although a 4-4-0T was produced for the East Kent Railway in 1857.

BELOW Designed by J.F. McIntosh and built at the company's St Rollox works in 1896, the Caledonian Railway 4-4-0 'Dunalastair' class caused a sensation in British railway circles because of the size and steaming capacity of its boiler. The class was developed over the next 20 years. No 142, shown here, was from the enlarged fourth series of 1904.

4-4-0T METROPOLITAN 1864

Tractive effort: 11,000lb (5034kg)

Axle load: 35,336lb (16 tonnes)

Cylinders: two 17x24in (432x609mm)

Driving wheels: 69in (175.25cm)

Heating surface: 1013.8 sq ft (94m²)

Superheater: n/a

Steam pressure: 130psi (9.16kg/cm²)

Grate area: 19sq ft (2.7 m²)

Fuel: Coal – 2240lb (1 tonne)

Water: 1000gall (1200 US) (4.54m³)

Total weight: 94,416lb (42.8 tonnes)

Overall length: 20ft 9in (6.32m)

Outside-cylinder 4-4-0s went on to be used by numerous lines, culminating in the Midland Compound and Southern 'Schools' classes, although both of these also possessed a third, inside cylinder. On the Great Western, with its more generous loading gauge, a series of outside-framed 4-4-0s was produced, from the days of Daniel Gooch into the 1930s. The first Gooch 4-4-0s were on rigid frames, however.

The inside-cylinder, express 4-4-0 was first produced by Thomas Wheatley on the NBR in 1871, and within a few years the type was widely employed by other designers. Its basic form was reproduced in many variations by every company of any size. With its sweeping curves, imposing yet handsome, uncluttered appearance and carefully handled details, it represented the peak of aesthetic design for the Victorian locomotive. As early as the 1840s, Joseph Locke – a practical engineer if not a locomotive man – had praised the accessibility of outside cylinders and motion. To most Victorian locomotive designers, however, there appeared to be something almost unseemly in exposing the 'works' to public view.

ABOVE The Metropolitan Railway's 4-4-0T, built by Beyer Peacock in 1864–70, was the first locomotive designed for underground running. The copper-lined pipes running from the cylinders to the side tanks were for conveying condensed steam, and the bridge-pipe and vent allowed vapour to exhaust from the tanks. The system often worked better in theory than in practice.

TANK ENGINES DEVELOP

During this period, a significant development was that of the tank engine. These had been known from the 1840s, and some early tender engines were converted to tank form, usually with a saddle tank fitted over the boiler. They remained relatively uncommon throughout the 1850s; however, by the 1890s, they almost out-numbered tender engines. Most services operated over relatively short distances with frequent stops, and for this work the tank engine was ideal. It could also be operated in reverse gear more satisfactorily than the tender locomotive and was independent of turntables. Well tank (within the frame), side and pannier tank types were also produced.

While the 0-6-0T was the most common type, the wheel arrangement of T-locos varied widely. Lines with longer commuter arteries, such as the London Tilbury & Southend and the Glasgow & South Western, built massive 4-6-4Ts (by the same designer, Robert Whitelegg); R.W. Urie of the South Western constructed a 4-8-0T; and the GWR had 2-8-0Ts for freight traffic. Some lines, such as the Rhymney Railway, had no need for anything other than tank engines. Sir John Aspinall's 2-4-2T for the L&YR numbered over 330, and the GW had over 800 of its 5700/8750 0-6-0T; only Ramsbottom's LNWR DX 0-6-0 outnumbered it as the most numerous single class, with 857 built.

LEFT This poster for the Highland Railway's London service is now at the preserved Monkwearmouth station of the North Eastern Railway; however, in the NER's heyday, the route it features would have been that of the 'enemy's', following the West Coast via Lancaster and Crewe.

0-6-0T TERRIER LBSCR 1872	
Tractive effort: 8400lb (3810kg)	
Axle load: 18,368lb (8.3 tonnes)	
Cylinders: two 13x20in (330x508mm)	
Driving wheels: 48in (122cm)	
Heating surface: 528sq ft (49m²)	
Superheater: n/a	
Steam pressure: 140psi (9.9kg/cm²)	
Grate area: 15sq ft (1.4m²)	
Fuel: Coal – 1120lb (0.5 tonne)	
Water: 500gall (600 US) (2.3m³)	
Total weight: 55,104lb (25 tonnes)	
Overall length: 12ft (3.65m)	

LEFT Broadside view of a Stroudley 0-6-0T 'Terrier' of the London Brighton & South Coast Railway, sold to the K&ESR in 1901.

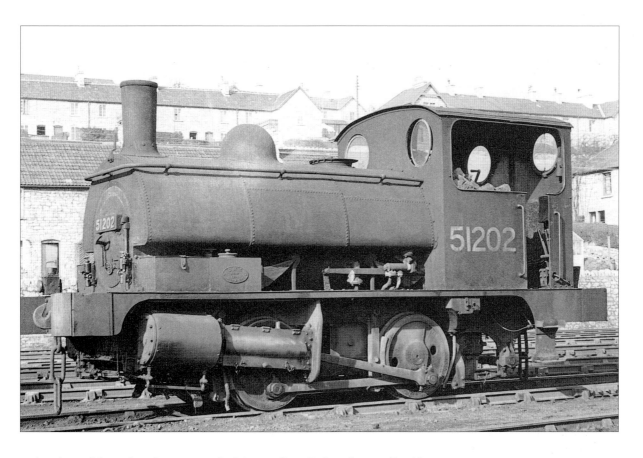

Another celebrated tank type was the Metropolitan Railway's 4-4-0T, with steam-condensing apparatus, built from 1864 by Beyer, Peacock & Co of Manchester to work on London's underground railway, the first in the world. Contrary to supposition, it was possible for a tank engine to cover a considerable distance without taking on coal or water. In 1908, engineers of the LNWR were astonished when, on an exchange trial, a 4-4-2T, of the LBSCR's class I3, ran from Rugby to Croydon without the need to refill its tanks. Its water and fuel consumption were markedly less than that of the LNWR 'Precursor' 4-4-0 against which it was being compared. A Brighton man is reputed to have said: 'We could have run on what she threw out of her chimney.'

The GWR was still a broad-gauge line, and it continued to build broad-gauge branches until 1877. But, even in 1852, the extension of its line from Oxford via Banbury to Birmingham was laid to mixed gauge. Eventually, its directors bowed to the inevitable. Although it could operate quite happily as a self-contained system, the business of transfer from broad- to standard-gauge for all intercompany traffic, particularly goods traffic, was expensive and time-consuming. As long-distance travel became more comfortable and holiday resorts grew in importance, there was more interest among the companies in promoting cross-country passenger services. The through carriage was also becoming popular. Attached to two or three trains in sequence, it provided a link on intertown routes where there was insufficient demand to warrant a whole direct train service. The Great Western had so far excluded itself from all this. At last, on 20 May 1892, the final broad-gauge train left Paddington for the West Country. Already much of the broad-gauge track had been narrowed. Now,

ABOVE The Lancashire & Yorkshire had many industrial sidings and canal-side tracks, and, like other companies, built very short wheelbase 'pug' tank engines to negotiate the tight curves. This one, surviving into British Railways' ownership as No 51202 of the London Midland Region, is a typical outside-cylindered, small-wheeled example of its kind. Because of their specialized but limited duties, many pugs had long working lives.

by 23 May, the task was completed. Long rows of old broad-gauge engines stood at Swindon waiting to be scrapped; more recent ones had been designed as 'convertibles' to fit the standard gauge. Deprived of its most distinctive aspect, however, the Great Western did not fall back into lassitude. Soon Swindon would show the world what it could do with locomotives built to the despised Stephenson 'cart-track' gauge.

RACING FOR PRESTIGE

Rivalry among railway companies was hardly news, but the 1890s turned it into news with the concept of railway 'races', and the newspapers of the day loved it. The West Coast route from Euston and the East Coast route from King's Cross – both to Aberdeen – converged at Kinnaber Junction, just north of Montrose, about 40 miles (64km) south of Aberdeen. North of here the line was owned by the Caledonian, and the North British had been granted running powers to Aberdeen. The West Coast companies – LNWR and Caledonian – and the East Coast – GNR, NER and NB – competed in

ABOVE The preserved GWR racer City of Truro on a special working at Banbury in 1992. Following refurbishment in the late 1980s, the veteran proved still to have a remarkable capacity for speed.

LEFT An unusual fitting on this GWR 0-6-0 pannier tank engine, No 2006 of Dean's 850 class, dating from 1881, was a bell, fitted American-style to the boiler top. This was for working on public roadways, on the tracks that lead to Birkenhead Docks.

August 1895 to achieve the fastest timing over the route, 541 miles (870.6km) for the former, 523.5 (842.5km) for the latter (the Forth Bridge had been opened in 1890). The first train offered to Kinnaber from the previous signal box on either line had the race sewn up. On the night of 20 August, both trains left London at 8 p.m. The West Coast train reached Kinnaber just four minutes ahead of its rival. Including numerous stops for engine-changing, it had maintained an average speed of 59.9mph (96.4km/h); the East Coast had maintained an average 57.8 (93km/h). Although the trains were very lightweight, it was a remarkable achievement. In the five weeks or so of the races, the London–Aberdeen time had been reduced by over three hours. In normal service, this margin was not maintained, but the races had shown what was possible. Indeed, at this time Britain led the world for the number of high-speed runs.

BELOW A broadside-on view of the Stirling GNR No 1 at speed, at the head of a train of vintage LNER carriages, between Doncaster and London, on the centenary of the Doncaster locomotive works, the 'Plant', in 1938.

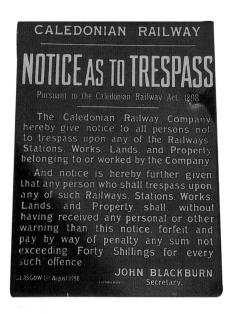

CALEDONIAN RAILWAY

NOTICE AS TO TRESPASS

Pursuant to the Caledonian Railway Act. 1898.

The Caledonian Railway Company hereby give notice to all persons not to trespass upon any of the Railways Stations. Works. Lands. and Property belonging to or worked by the Company

And notice is hereby further given that any person who shall trespass upon any of such Railways. Stations. Works. Lands. and Property. shall. without having received any personal or other warning than this notice. forfeit and pay by way of penalty any sum not exceeding Forty Shillings for every such offence.

JOHN BLACKBURN
Secretary.

GLASGOW 1st August 1898.

Rivalry also broke out in the next decade on the lines from London to the West, where the LSWR and the GWR vied for the honour of transporting passengers and mails from Europe-bound transatlantic liners pausing at Plymouth. Both companies had termini there, and the two routes intersected each other at Exeter. Unlike the routes to Scotland, these were one-company lines all the way – 247.2 miles (397.8km) for the GWR and 230 miles (370.1km) for the LSWR – and the two CMEs, Dugald Drummond of the LSWR and George Churchward of the GWR, took a personal interest. Drummond himself went on at least one of the runs; Churchward left this to G.H. Flewellyn, a senior locomotive inspector. But he gave him the following typically Churchwardian instruction: 'Withhold any attempt at a maximum speed record till I give you the word. Then you can go and break your bloody neck!' It was on an 'Ocean Mail' special, on 9 May 1904, that the GWR 4-4-0 *City of Truro* attained a speed exceeding 100mph (160.9km/h) for the first time on British metals, racing down Wellington Bank towards Taunton.

On 1 July 1906, an American boat-train's horrific crash at Salisbury, caused by excessive speed, put an end to these excitements. Public opinion moved with its usual rapidity from enthusiasm for speed to fear of disaster. Maximum speed attempts were ruled out, and speed restrictions that had been winked at were again firmly enforced.

LEFT Trespass notices were there not only to warn people off, but to absolve the railway company from any legal claim by persons injured by straying on the line. An early law (1845) compelled all main-line railways to be fenced off.

BELOW The combined wheel-splashers were a trademark of the North Eastern Railway's 4-4-0s. Wilson Worsdell's R class of 1899 became LNER D20, and No 1904 is seen here at West Hartlepool. Although the engines underwent considerable alteration in the 1930s, the class survived as late as 1959.

IMPROVING STANDARDS

By the 1890s, the railways had emerged from the trough of public disesteem. Gradually, things had improved. Although some companies, such as the Highland, still provided wooden seats in third class, and some trains still seemed to crawl across the landscape and stand still for long, unexplained periods at country junctions, the general standard had improved considerably. By this time, corridor coaches were the norm on long-distance trains. Sleeping cars and dining cars had been introduced. Signalling and braking had been vastly improved. Comparative studies such as Foxwell and Farrer's *Express Trains, English and Foreign* of 1889 revealed how British railways were superior to those on the Continent, and not only in speed and frequency. In Britain, 93 per cent of the express trains carried third-class passengers; in France, Bavaria and Italy, the proportion was only 27 per cent. There was a new awareness that British trains could compare with the best that the rest of the world had to offer and that the railway companies could be much worse than they in fact were.

ABOVE The first Pullman cars in Britain were introduced from the USA by the Midland Railway in 1873, when sleeping and parlour cars were used on its new Anglo-Scottish main line via Leeds and Dumfries. This later example shows the distinctive styling and colour scheme, and the fine detail, of these sumptuous cars.

3 • The Big Four

The twentieth century brings new challenges to the steam railway – world war, the advent of motor competition and the need for reorganization on a massive scale. It also sees the supreme achievement of steam-generated speed and power in Britain, with the magnificent A4 and 'Coronation' class locomotives.

LEFT R.J. Billinton designed the E4-class 0-6-2 radial tank engine for the London Brighton & South Coast Railway in 1898. 'Radial' refers to the bar allowing the pony wheels to adjust independently to sharp curves. Restored class member No 473 *Birch Grove* is seen here on a winter day at Horsted Keynes on the Bluebell Railway.

OPPOSITE Preserved LMS 'Jinty' 3F 0-6-0T No 7298 at Glyndyfrdwy, on the Llangollen Railway. The origins of this type go back to the Lancashire & Yorkshire Railway; although primarily a goods shunting engine, it was also used on passenger services on the Somerset & Dorset line and in some other areas.

AROUND THE END OF THE NINETEENTH CENTURY, important innovations began to appear in locomotive design. British mechanical engineers were a tough breed: they had to be large-scale industrial managers as well as engine designers. Men such as Sir John Aspinall of the Lancashire & Yorkshire Railway planned and laid out large workshops (Horwich in his case) and controlled large numbers of men. His contemporary, Dugald Drummond of the LSWR, with works at Nine Elms and Eastleigh, and responsibility for locomotive running, also built his own private engine car (known to his staff as 'the Bug') to cruise over his far-flung domain. But these men, for all their power, did not dictate company policy. The demands being made by the traffic departments were ever greater, and the number-crunchers in the financial departments who desired operational cost-effectiveness were increasingly vocal and influential. Engine designers who had grown up with the 4-2-2 and 0-6-0 were being forced to consider much larger and more powerful tractive units for both goods and passenger working. Aspinall (later to became general manager of the line) was also a locomotive designer of distinction, whose 4-4-2 'Highflyers' romped through the Pennines with business

expresses. In the bigger companies, all engineers had to face the 'big engine' challenge. In 1896, John F. McIntosh, chief mechanical engineer of the Caledonian Railway, created intense interest in railway circles when he introduced his new 'Dunalastair' 4-4-0. Still in the classic inside-cylinder style, it was distinguished by a boiler of 4ft 8in (142.2cm) diameter, the largest yet seen. An ex-driver, McIntosh produced an engine that was simple to operate and had ample steam-raising capacity. The 'Dunalastairs' did excellent service, and most engineers followed McIntosh's example.

The chief mechanical engineer with by far the largest locomotive stable was Francis W. Webb of the LNWR. The famous earlier designs of his long reign (1871–1903), the 'Cauliflower' 0-6-0 and the 'Jumbo' 2-4-0, were straightforward machines that responded well to hard driving. Soon, however, Webb became fatally interested in compound working. In this, the steam was used twice over, first at high pressure, then – exhausted from one set of cylinders into another – at lower pressure. In theory, it was a more efficient use of motive power and fuel. In practice, however, Webb's successive compound

ABOVE This Caledonian Railway 0-6-0 was built by J.F. McIntosh in 1899, at St Rollox Works. Although essentially a freight class, the first 17, including the preserved No 828, shown here at Aviemore, were painted in Caledonian blue and used on Clyde coast passenger services.

OPPOSITE One of J.F. Webb's 0-6-0s, called 'Cauliflowers' because of the LNWR coat of arms painted on the middle wheel-splasher, takes a train of coal wagons over the Settle and Carlisle line. These simple-expansion engines were much preferred by crews to Webb's compound locomotives.

LEFT Sir John Aspinall's Lancashire & Yorkshire Class L1 4-2-2 'Highflyer' of 1899 was Britain's second Atlantic type and was renowned for speed on the long-distance commuter lines radiating from Manchester.

designs were tricky to drive and often temperamental in operation. On frequent occasions, they were seen attempting to start off with each pair of driving wheels revolving in opposite directions. It is remarkable that Sir Richard Moon tolerated what was undoubtedly an unnecessarily expensive and wasteful practice for so long – an indication of how much, even on the North Western, the CME was an unquestionable autocrat in his own domain. Webb's successors, George Whale and C.J. Bowen-Cooke, scrapped his engines as fast as they could and produced a range of simple-expansion locomotives that were vastly more reliable.

SCIENTIFIC INNOVATIONS

Part of the real shape of things to come was displayed on the Highland Railway, where in 1894 David Jones introduced the first 4-6-0 locomotives used in Britain, the very successful 'Big Goods'. But the main and continuing centre of innovation was Swindon, mechanical headquarters of the GWR. Here George Jackson Churchward, appointed locomotive superintendent in 1902, brought scientific principles to bear on design and construction. Unlike most of his peers, who – with unjustifiable arrogance and complacency – regarded British methods as naturally best, he was keen to learn and benefit from foreign practice, especially that of the Northern Railway of France, where the designer Alfred De Glehn had built some remarkable 4-4-2 Atlantic-type compound locomotives. The Great Western purchased

---

0-6-0 CAULIFLOWER LNWR 1880

Tractive effort: 15,000lb (6800kg)

Axle load: 24,897lb (11.3 tonnes)

Cylinders: two 18x24in (457x609mm)

Driving wheels: 61½in (156cm)

Heating surface: 1208sq ft (112m²)

Superheater: n/a

Steam pressure: 140psi (9.9kg/cm²)

Grate area: 17sq ft (1.6m²)

Fuel: Coal – 8960lb (4 tonnes)

Water: 3250gall (3903 US) (14.75m³)

Total weight: 74,704lb (33.9 tonnes)

Overall length: 15ft 6in (4.73m)

three of these between 1903 and 1905, played with them intensively, and incorporated many features into Swindon practice, although not the compounding. Churchward found that the 'simple' use of steam answered his requirements effectively. The only British company to build really successful compound engines was the Midland, where a succession of engineers – Robinson, Smith and Deeley – built successive generations of the 4-4-0 'Midland Compound' that ran almost all the company's express trains.

The Midland was unusual in this respect. By the early 1900s, the 10-wheeler was regarded as essential by most lines for hauling mainline passenger trains. In many cases, the preferred version was the Atlantic, whose 4-4-2 wheel arrangement allowed for a wider firebox than the 4-6-0. The first British Atlantics were built by H.A. Ivatt on the Great Northern in 1898 and were known as 'Klondykes', as the Alaskan gold rush was on at the time. In 1902, Ivatt introduced a larger-boilered version, the first of which, No 251, is preserved along with the first 'Klondyke', *Henry Oakley*. The Lancashire & Yorkshire, Great Central, London Brighton & South Coast and North British, among others, also favoured the Atlantic for mainline services. The 4-6-0's advantage over the Atlantic lay in its greater tractive power, with the coupled wheels bearing more of the engine's weight.

ABOVE After the 1923 Grouping, some engines were transferred to new territory. Many Midland 4-4-0s went to the Glasgow & South Western Railway. This one is on a Kilmarnock– Dumfries stopping train.

4-4-2 HENRY OAKLEY GNR 1898

Tractive effort: 18,000lb (8160kg)

Axle load: 35,840lb (16.25 tonnes)

Cylinders: two 18¾x24in (476x609mm)

Driving wheels: 79½in (202cm)

Heating surface: 1442sq ft (134m²)

Superheater: n/a

Steam pressure: 175psi (12.3kg/cm²)

Grate area: 26.75sq ft (2.5m²)

Fuel: Coal – 14,320lb (6.5 tonnes)

Water: 3500gall (4203 US) (16m³)

Total weight: 129,920lb (58.9 tonnes)

Overall length: 26ft 4in (8.03m)

Not all designers succeeded with this type. Dugald Drummond, after a series of excellent and elegant 4-4-0 types, produced large, ponderous-looking 4-6-0s on the LSWR, including the aptly nicknamed 'Paddleboxes', the performance of which was generally less than sparkling. McIntosh, pioneer of the big boiler, produced a handsome inside-cylindered 4-6-0 for the Caledonian's heavy Anglo-Scottish expresses. The most famous was the 'Cardean' class, which performed well, but not outstandingly. It seemed that it was a hard type to get right, although Highland 'Castles' and GW 'Stars' demonstrated, in their different areas, that the 4-6-0 could be extremely successful. On the LSWR and the Caledonian, however, the older 4-4-0s were to outlive their bigger shed-mates by many years.

ALL CHANGE

On all lines, boilers became bigger, their pressure increased, chimneys and domes shrank, as the designers coped with fitting more power into the tight British loading gauge.

ABOVE Britain's first Atlantic locomotive was the GNR's *Henry Oakley* of 1898, designed by H.A. Ivatt. These 4-4-2s were known as 'Klondykes' after the gold rush of the time.

OPPOSITE A shunting engine and crew pose for the camera. LMS 2F Fowler dock tank 0-6-0T 11275, built in 1928, is in sparkling condition. Note the hooked shunting pole, used to attach and detach couplings while the wagons were on the move: a job requiring skill and muscle.

The number of driving wheels increased. 0-8-0 locomotives were introduced on the North Eastern, 2-8-0s on the GWR and GNR, to replace the old double-heading on coal and minerals trains. Traffic was still expanding, and, despite the increase in power, the total number of engines in use continued to rise. The continuing increase in freight traffic led to the building of large marshalling yards, with the innovation of hump shunting. At Feltham in West London (LSWR), Stratford in East London (GER) and Wath upon Dearne (GCR), among other places, vast arrays of sidings were laid out. Large tank-engine types were designed to move long wagon trains: on the London & South Western, R.W. Urie's 4-8-0T of class G16 was rated as amongst the company's most powerful engine types.

Changes on one front, in this case the greater weight and length of locomotives, demanded changes on others. Tender engines had to be turned at the end of their run, and, unless there was a convenient triangular layout, this meant using a turntable. Turntables built in 1880 to fit 4-4-0s might not be long enough for a 4-6-0 in 1905. New ones were often needed, and other engine shed facilities, such as coaling platforms, also had to be altered or extended. A distinctive feature of the steam railway was the water column at the platform ends of many stations, with its accompanying tank set on brick or metal supports. At some places where double-headed trains passed regularly, such as Crianlarich

BELOW The Caledonian Railway built the 'Cardean' class inside-cylinder 4-6-0s in 1906 to haul mainline passenger expresses. *Cardean* itself was the regular engine on the Glasgow-Carlisle section of the 'Corridor', precursor of the 'Royal Scot'. The big eight-wheel tender allowed engines to run non-stop between Carlisle and Perth (151 miles/243km).

on the West Highland, these columns were set in pairs so that the train and pilot engines could take on water at the same time.

Heavier engines and trains, and higher speeds, made new demands on the permanent way. Major bridges had usually been built with such strength that they coped easily (some of Brunel's brick bridges are still in use), but many smaller bridges had to be strengthened. The trackbed and rails also had to be of sufficient support and strength. Sleepers had usually been laid on a cinder base, thriftily using a railway by-product. Now, main lines were laid on quarried stone chips. There was concern not only about clearances, but also about the 'hammer-blow' inflicted on the rails

by driving wheels, and new locomotive types had to be passed by the civil engineer before they were allowed to run. This caused a major row on the Highland Railway in 1916, when the civil engineer flatly refused to let the newly delivered big 'River'-class 4-6-0s set wheel on the line, and all six had to be sold off to the Caledonian.

Into the twentieth century, new steam-powered lines were still being built. Some of these were remote, such as the extensions to Mallaig and Kyle of Lochalsh in the western Highlands. But just before the end of the nineteenth century, the last main line into London (until the 21st-century Channel Tunnel link) was completed with the arrival of the Great Central Railway at Marylebone Station in March 1899. Known until August 1897 as the Manchester, Sheffield & Lincolnshire Railway, the Great Central was run with style and verve (its founding father, Sir Edward Watkin, had planned a Channel tunnel). But London and the East Midlands were already well connected via the Great Northern and Midland Railways. The speed and comfort of the GC expresses, drawn by J.G. Robinson's handsome Atlantics, the 'Jersey Lilies', attracted custom, but their traffic and revenues were always far less than those of their rivals.

THE MODERN FACE OF STEAM

By around 1912, it could be said that the modern steam locomotive had arrived. All the essential features were present. It is worth pointing out that, although Britain produced the first locomotives, some of the most important technical features came from

ABOVE CR No 903 *Cardean* leaves Glasgow with a southbound express. These locomotives had their own full-time drivers, who were also responsible for care and routine maintenance.

BELOW From 1923 until the end of steam, the majority of Great Western fast passenger services were handled by the 'Castle'-class 4-6-0s, designed by C.B. Collett very much in the tradition of G.J. Churchward.

elsewhere. A vital and universally used addition to efficiency was the steam injector, developed by the French engineer Henri Giffard in 1859. This device forced water from the tender into the boiler against the internal steam pressure. The valve gear which was used on most modern engines was based on that devised by the Belgian Egide Walschaerts, in 1844–48. Another Belgian, Alfred Belpaire, developed the flat-topped firebox which was used on many engines, from the 1880s up to the British Railways standard types. Although British engineers had tried superheating at

various times in the nineteenth century, it was the German Schmidt superheater, developed in the early 1900s, which provided by far the best solution. The superheater took steam from the boiler and led it through a series of intensely hot flues, pushing up its temperature and expanding its volume, and so enabling less steam to do more work when it passed into the cylinders. It vastly improved locomotive performance.

ABOVE The two-cylinder LNER B1 class, seen here in preserved BR 62005 at Goathland on the North Yorks Moors Railway.

4-6-2 THE GREAT BEAR GWR 1908

Tractive effort: 29,430lb (13,346kg)

Axle load: 45,808lb (20.8 tonnes)

Cylinders: four 15x26in (381x660mm)

Driving wheels: 80½in (204.5cm)

Heating surface: 2831.5sq ft (263m²)

Superheater: 545sq ft (50.5 m²)

Steam pressure: 225psi (15.8kg/cm²)

Grate area: 41.8sq ft (3.9 m²)

Fuel: Coal – 13,440lb (6.1 tonnes)

Water: 3500gall (4203 US) (16m³)

Total weight: 218,400lb (99 tonnes)

Overall length: 34ft 6in (10.52m)

From then until the end of steam traction, improvements were a matter of detail and scale.

The new order was first revealed on the Great Western. Even before he assumed supreme command, the influence of Churchward was seen on the GW 'Atbara' 4-4-0s of 1898, but it was with the 'Cities' of 1903 that the hallmarks of a tapered boiler – an almost square-topped firebox and no dome – became familiar. In 1906 came the first of the celebrated four-cylinder 4-6-0 'Star' class, *North Star* (built first as an Atlantic), the direct ancestor of the later 'Castles' and 'Kings'. Like them, it was intended for express passenger work, but equally significant were the two-cylinder 'Saints', from which the LMS 'Black Five' was descended. The GWR engines were relatively expensive to build: when challenged by the company's directors on why it was that the LNWR could build three 4-6-0s for the price of two GW 'Stars', Churchward is reputed to have replied: 'Because one of mine could pull two of their bloody things backwards!' Interchange trials arranged by the LNWR in 1910 proved the superiority of the GW engines beyond doubt. C.J. Bowen-Cooke's new 'George V'-class 4-4-0 *Worcestershire*

ABOVE Churchward's *The Great Bear*, shown here on the 'Cheltenham Tea Car Express', was Britain's first Pacific-type locomotive (1908) and the only one ever built by the GWR.

OPPOSITE A tank locomotive with express headlamps: preserved ex-LNER Class N2 0-6-2, in BR livery as 69523, is seen on the Great Central Railway. With condensing pipes for working in tunnel sections, the class was designed in 1920 to work suburban traffic north and south from King's Cross.

was wholly outclassed by the GWR *Lode Star.* The situation would be repeated in 1925 on the LNER and in 1928 on the LMS.

Nevertheless, on the LNWR, Bowen-Cooke and his predecessor George Whale had revolutionized the motive-power scene since 1903. One writer has called engines such as the 'Precursors' of 1904 and the 'George Vs' the Tin Lizzies of railway engines: cheap to build, straightforward to drive, uncomplicated to maintain, they hammered along with plenty of noise, rattle and smoke, but they had plenty of steam and speed too, and were solidly reliable. The enginemen loved them. Bowen-Cooke's four-cylinder express 4-6-0 of 1913, the 'Claughton', sought to combine some of the virtues of Swindon and Crewe; however, despite some very good test performances, its overall record was undistinguished, and the design was not developed by the LMS after 1923.

In 1908, Churchward also built the first British 4-6-2, or Pacific, locomotive, *The Great Bear.* It remained a one-off and was later converted to 4-6-0. The great era of the Pacific was yet to come, and its greatest engineers, Nigel Gresley and William Stanier, were still young men in 1908, working on the designs of others (in Stanier's case, those of Churchward).

BELOW Designed to work on the West Highland Railway, the preserved *The Great Marquess*, one of Sir Nigel Gresley's K4-class 2-6-0s of 1937, seen on the Freshfield bank, Bluebell Railway. The brief was to produce an engine with relatively light axle loading and considerable power. Speed was not a major concern.

SPECIAL WAR SERVICES

When World War I broke out in August 1914, the railways of Britain were immediately placed under government control. For the first time, a single central authority, the Railway Executive Committee, was imposed over the 120 operating companies. Around a third of the railways' male staff volunteered for war service, and the phenomenon of the lady porter and signalwoman appeared. Railway workshops switched to building tanks and making munitions. Vast numbers of special trains were run, the most celebrated being the 'Misery', which ran every night between Euston and Thurso carrying naval personnel to and from the Grand Fleet's base at Scapa Flow. The nickname 'Misery' was heartfelt. It took more than 22 hours for its journey of 728 miles (1172km).

BELOW In 1900, James Holden of the Great Eastern Railway introduced the 'Claud Hamilton' class 4-4-0 for express services, including its longest non-stop run, 131 miles (242km) between Liverpool Street and North Walsham, 'The Norfolk Coast Express'. The original engine is seen here on exhibition in LNER colours.

Between 1914 and 1919, intensive traffic and reduced maintenance took a heavy toll on the railways. At the end of the war, most were in a decrepit state, short of equipment and money. All were owed large sums by the government, following their provision of special war services. Despite many protestations of gratitude for the companies' work, the government proved to be a slow, reluctant and incomplete payer, and some companies, including the North British, almost collapsed while waiting their due. Disgruntled railway staff held their

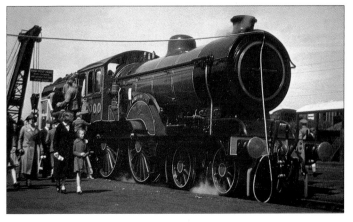

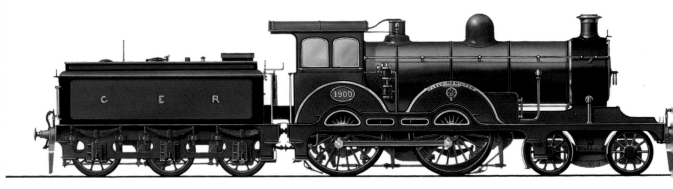

first national strike in September–October 1919. To the fury of the companies, the government granted an eight-hour working day and substantial pay rises.

In 1919, for the first time, the British government included a Minister of Transport, Sir Eric Geddes, once deputy general manager of the North Eastern Railway. His presence indicated the intention to have a national transport policy, but this did not come about. To the central controllers, however, it had seemed clear that to have more than 120 railway companies in a relatively small country was wildly uneconomic, as well as highly inefficient. Each one, however small, had its hierarchy of officers, its workshops and depots. Often competing with one another for the same traffic, many had little chance of remaining profitable in the postwar world. Already the electric tramcar had caused the abandonment of many suburban services; now the petrol-engined bus and truck were coming on to the scene in large numbers. Throughout the war, the railways, under government regulation, were refused permission to increase their freight charges. In 1920, when they at last went up, they nearly doubled overnight. As common carriers, the railways were forced to publish a scale of charges. The road hauliers could charge

ABOVE The GER made numerous experiments with oil rather than coal fuel, and a number of the 'Claud Hamilton' 4-4-0s were fitted out as oil burners, with tank tenders. With North Sea oil still undiscovered, coal was always the cheaper option for British steam railways.

LEFT Another preserved example of the once-ubiquitous 0-6-0 type is the North British *Maude*, built in 1891 and classed J31 by the LNER. Rebuilt in 1915, it went to France for army work in 1917–18, then worked in Scotland until 1966. It is now on the Bo'ness and Kinneil Railway.

what they liked and found it easy to undercut the railways. It was clear that some ratio-nalization of the railways was necessary.

AMALGAMATION AND THE RAILWAYS ACT

The railways passed out of government control on 15 August 1921. Four days later, the Railways Act came into force, enjoining the amalgamation of all railway companies into regional groups by June 1923. An Amalgamation Tribunal was set up to coordi-nate matters and resolve disputes. A number of amalgamations (called the Grouping) followed swiftly, while discussion still went on about the eventual shape of things. By January 1923, however, the work was completed. Four great railway companies replaced the previous multiplicity. Of the larger constituents, the London, Midland & Scottish Railway embraced the LNWR, L&Y, Midland, Caledonian, GSWR and Highland. The London & North Eastern Railway comprised the GN, GC, GER, NER and NB. The Southern Railway comprised the LSWR, LBSCR and SECR. The Great Western Railway alone retained its former title, with its empire now enlarged by all the Welsh companies, such as the Cambrian and the Taff Vale. Only three joint systems – the Cheshire Lines, the Somerset & Dorset and the Midland & Great Northern – and a handful of very small independent standard-gauge lines were outside the ambit of the Railways Act; they continued to be run as before. The Big Four would last until the railways were nationalized in 1948.

ABOVE The Southern Railway's 'King Arthur' class of 4-6-0s, 'Knights of the Turntable', was designed by Richard Maunsell in 1925 to provide the company's basic express passenger traction. Preserved No 777 *Sir Lamiel* was always one of the star performers and is seen here at Rothley as BR 30777.

The amalgamations and takeovers were not accomplished without argument, difficulty and even heartache. The old companies had often engendered fierce loyalty among their staff, together with contempt for rivals. The problems were particularly acute in the newly formed LMS, the biggest single railway business in the world, where ancient hatreds between LNWR and Midland still flourished. One-time chiefs became divisional heads, answerable to men who had been their commercial or mechanical rivals. Was the proud engineering tradition of Darlington to bow to that of Doncaster? Or Crewe to Derby? The answer was yes – but it took time for the new scheme of things to settle down. Traffic managers had to decide between competing routes in some cases. The Southern, now with two routes to Portsmouth, downgraded the old Mid-Sussex line through Horsham in favour of the former LSWR direct line via Guildford and received such a blast of bad publicity that it became the first railway company to set up a modern-style public relations department to put its own side of the story.

The Great Western apart, it took some years for an *esprit de corps* to emerge among the new companies. The almost family atmosphere of such lines as the GSWR and the

OPPOSITE In BR livery, Sir William Stanier's ex-LMS Pacific *City of Lichfield* puts out full power on the climb to Beattock Summit with the down 'Royal Scot.'

BELOW One of two preserved LNER three-cylinder class Q 0-8-0s, seen here at Thomason Foss on North Yorkshire Moors Railway.

Hull & Barnsley could not be preserved. Staff relations were poor, with managements refusing to talk to the trades unions. Although the new chiefs tried to familiarize themselves with their regional outposts, they were inevitably seen as remote figures. On the LMS, Lord Stamp, the chairman and general manager from 1927, who had a carriage fitted out to take him round the system, was regarded with nervous hostility by the staff. His visits were seen as 'sacking tours'. Stamp's great ambition, in the tradition of Sir Richard Moon, was to reduce the costs of the company by standardization and by economies – and if the latter meant grubby trains and unpolished engines, then so be it.

BELOW Preserved LNER class A2 Pacific 60532 *Blue Peter* takes the 10.15 Leicester–Loughborough on the restored Great Central main line – the 20-mile (33.8km) trip rather easier than its original service.

HARD HIT BY THE DEPRESSION

For eight years from 1929, the railways suffered, like the rest of the country, from the slump in trade and industry known as the Great Depression. Pay for all grades was reduced by 2.5 per cent in 1929. The basic traffic in coal, iron ore and steel fell disastrously. Many staff were laid off. With reduced revenues, there was less opportunity for new investment. Although it was also a decade of technical progress, with high-performance locomotive types appearing, there was less replacement of veteran types than would otherwise have been the case.

4-6-0 ROYAL SCOT LMS 1927

Tractive effort: 34,000 lb (15,420kg)
Axle load: 47,040lb (21.3 tonnes)
Cylinders: three 18x26in (457x660mm)
Driving wheels: 81in (205.75cm)
Heating surface: 2081sq ft (193.3m²)
Superheater: 445sq ft (41.3m²)
Steam pressure: 250psi (17.6kg/cm²)
Grate area: 31.2sq ft (2.9m²)
Fuel: Coal – 11,200lb (5 tonnes)
Water: 3500gall (4203 US) (16m³)
Total weight: 190,400lb (86.3 tonnes)
Overall length: 27ft 6in (8.38m)

This was even more true of the carriage and wagon stock. The typical goods wagon or van remained a basic four-wheeler without provision for automatic or continuous brakes. The industrial recovery of the later 1930s was led by new 'light' industries, running on electrical power and situated with an eye to road, rather than rail, links. The rail connection was no longer vital.

The railway companies, like other big businesses, found that it was desirable to cultivate a public image that was sometimes at variance with their actual average performance. The

ABOVE The original LMS 'Royal Scot' type 4-6-0 of 1927 was an immensely impressive machine, though its subsequent rebuilding in the 1940s made it a far more effective and efficient one.

BELOW Rebuilt 'Royal Scot' No 46102, *Black Watch*, sets off from the now-closed Edinburgh Princes Street station with a local train for Glasgow Central.

natural way to do this was by focusing public attention on a select number of prestige routes and trains. All of them did this to some extent. The Southern introduced the 'Atlantic Coast Express', from Waterloo to the north Cornwall resorts, on 19 July 1926. In 1929, it inaugurated the all-Pullman 'Golden Arrow' service on the London–Dover–Paris route. The LMS ran many named trains including the longest-distance scheduled service, the overnight 'Royal Highlander' from Inverness to Euston. Its crack train was the 10 a.m. 'Royal Scot' from Euston to Glasgow and Edinburgh, long known to operating staff as 'The Corridor', as it had been one of the first corridor trains. For no very obvious

LONDON, MIDLAND AND SCOTTISH
RAILWAY: MAJOR LINES AND
BRANCHES AT 1 JANUARY 1923

London, Midland and
Scottish Railway

Joint Railways

reason, the GWR picked the town of Cheltenham for its fastest train, 'The Cheltenham Spa Express', which began in 1923 and was popularly known as the 'Cheltenham Flyer'. For a period, this was the fastest train in the world, with a scheduled run between Swindon and Paddington of 77.3 miles (124.4km) in 70 minutes. Its best recorded time was made on 2 June 1932, with an average of 81.7mph (131.5km/h). The most famous of the named trains was the LNER's 10 a.m. King's Cross–Edinburgh, the 'Flying Scotsman'. Like the 'Royal Scot', it had a long pedigree. From 1 May 1928, this train

made the longest non-stop run in the world, with no scheduled halt between start and finish of its journey. Despite economic uncertainty and ever greater road competition, Britain's railway companies could thus claim to lead the world in a number of ways.

ABOVE The GWR 2-8-2T of 1934 is a conversion of two earlier 2-8-0T types, 4200 and 5200, built around the time of World War I.

RATIONALIZATION

Rationalization and reallocation of rolling stock and locomotives often improved services. Lines which had still been using wooden six-wheel vehicles from the previous century were equipped with steel bogie coaches; even if these were second-hand from elsewhere, they were a great improvement. Locomotives sometimes ran far from their one-time haunts. Midland Compounds on the old Caledonian and GSW lines gave sterling performances, often with loads far greater than originally envisaged for them.

BELOW G.J. Churchward's two-cylinder 'Saint' class, introduced in 1907.

The LNER built a new batch of 4-4-0 'Directors' of the Great Central's design for use in Scotland. There was still no national policy for locomotive design. Each of the Big Four kept its own locomotive works, although the smaller ones were normally reduced to repair and maintenance depots.

An interesting difference in philosophy emerged between the designers of the LMS and the LNER. Under the dominating influence of Lord Stamp, the LMS aim was to construct locomotives which could be employed anywhere on a system that stretched from Wick to Bournemouth. Gresley, chief mechanical engineer of the LNER from 1923, believed in matching locomotive types to particular routes. Whilst the LMS policy had greater logic behind it, the LNER's gave it a more varied and distinctive locomotive stock and was much more beloved of railway enthusiasts. (Prior to the introduction of Gresley's Beyer-Garratt locomotive in 1925, the most striking example of an engine built for a specific route was the Midland's solitary 0-10-0, known as 'Big

BELOW The Southern Railway's four-cylinder 'Lord Nelson' class 4-6-0 appeared in 1926 and was in mainline service for 30 years. All were refitted with wide chimney and multiple-blast. In this 1948 scene, No 861 *Lord Anson* heads out of Victoria with an express.

LEFT The Great Central 'Director' class 4-4-0s were introduced by J.G. Robinson in 1915 and handled that company's relatively lightweight but fast expresses on the main line from Marylebone to Sheffield. They mark the final development of the characteristically British inside-cylinder 4-4-0. One member of the class, No 506 *Butler-Henderson*, survives in preservation.

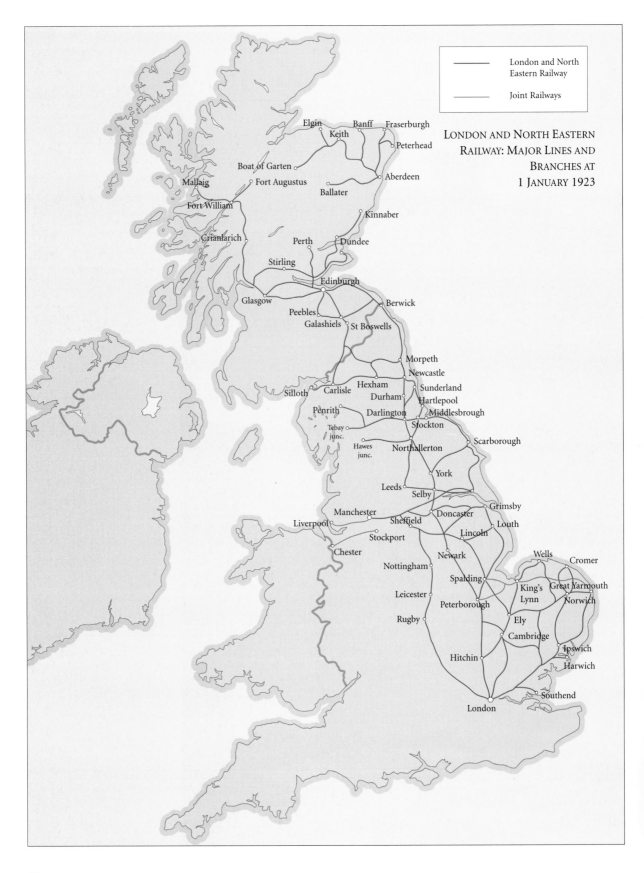

London and North Eastern Railway

Joint Railways

LONDON AND NORTH EASTERN
RAILWAY: MAJOR LINES AND
BRANCHES AT
1 JANUARY 1923

Elgin · Banff · Fraserburgh
Keith
Peterhead
Boat of Garten
Aberdeen
Mallaig · Fort Augustus
Ballater
Fort William
Kinnaber
Crianlarich
Perth · Dundee
Stirling
Edinburgh
Glasgow
Berwick
Peebles
Galashiels · St Boswells
Morpeth
Newcastle
Hexham · Sunderland
Silloth · Carlisle · Durham · Hartlepool
Penrith · Darlington · Middlesbrough
Tebay junc. · Stockton
Hawes junc. · Northallerton · Scarborough
York
Leeds
Selby
Grimsby
Manchester · Doncaster
Liverpool · Sheffield · Louth
Lincoln
Stockport
Chester · Newark · Wells · Cromer
Nottingham · King's Lynn · Great Yarmouth
Spalding · Norwich
Leicester · Peterborough · Ely
Rugby · Cambridge
Ipswich
Hitchin · Harwich
London · Southend

Emma' or 'Big Bertha', which spent its entire career from 1920 to 1956 banking trains up the Lickey Incline.)

Each company set about building new locomotives, and the new urge for favourable publicity was soon followed by some of the old rivalries. Each new express type had to be bigger or more powerful. This trend began on the Great Western in 1923 with the appearance of the first 'Castle', *Caerphilly Castle,* hailed as the most powerful express engine in Britain. Designed by C.B. Collett, Churchward's successor from 1923, it was in every way in the Churchward tradition. In 1926, when R.E.L. Maunsell introduced the 'Lord Nelson' four-cylinder 4-6-0, the Southern's publicity machine trumpeted it as 'the most powerful passenger engine in the country'. In 1927, Collett brought out the 'King' class, the theoretical tractive effort of which was slightly greater and thus won back the accolade.

ABOVE The Midland Railway's 0-10-0 was a one-off, built in 1919 to bank heavy trains up the 1:38 Lickey Incline of its Bristol-Birmingham main line. Common in many other countries, ten-coupled engines were an extreme rarity on British lines until the 'Austerity' 2-10-0 of World War II.

LEFT Preserved GWR Class 43xx 2-6-0 7325 at Kidderminster, Severn Valley Railway. Great Western 'Moguls' go back to pre-1914, but this one was built in 1932. Although it was intended as a mixed-traffic engine, fast goods services were its main task.

2-6-0 5P4F CRAB LMS 1926

Tractive effort: 27,000lb (12,245kg)
Axle load: 21,280lb (9.6 tonnes)
Cylinders: two 21x26in (533x660mm)
Driving wheels: 66in (167.5cm)
Heating surface: 1412sq ft (131.2m²)
Superheater: 308sq ft (28.6m²)
Steam pressure: 180psi (12.7kg/cm²)
Grate area: 27.5sq ft (2.5m²)
Fuel: Coal – 11,200lb (5 tonnes)
Water: 3500gall (4203 US) (16m³)
Total weight: 150,080lb (68 tonnes)
Overall length: 25ft 6in (7.77m)

The LMS – after having gone through a succession of CMEs, and having done nothing more enterprising than build more of the Midland Compounds and some smaller mixed-traffic engines such as the sturdy Horwich-designed 'Crab' 2-6-0 – found itself short of powerful express locomotives in 1928. A compound Pacific was in an advanced state of design at Derby, but the LNWR faction, with memories of Webb, opposed this plan. A GW 'Castle' was borrowed, unknown to Fowler, and showed that a simple-expansion 4-6-0 could keep time with the West Coast expresses. Top

ABOVE The L&Y 'Crab' 2-6-0, of 1922, was a useful general-purpose engine, showing that its designers had learned from the failure and successful rebuilding of the 4-6-0 type that preceded it. No 42765 is seen here on Summerseat viaduct, East Lancashire Railway.

management was convinced; the Pacific was abandoned and an express 4-6-0 was urgently demanded. Despite his command of major works at Crewe, Horwich, Glasgow and Derby, the CME, Sir Henry Fowler, turned to the privately owned North British Locomotive Company in Glasgow for the rapid production of 50 of the imposing three-cylinder 'Royal Scot' 4-6-0, which was to a very large extent based on the 'Lord Nelson' design. This engine's claim to promotional fame was a boiler pressure of 250lb (113kg). All these various express types performed their basic task adequately,

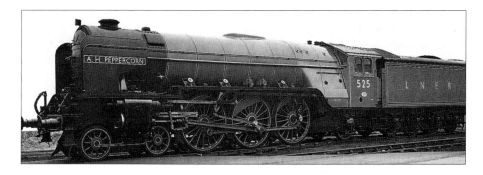

LEFT The LNER's last fling: A2 Pacific No 525 *A.H. Peppercorn*, named after its designer, stands newly finished at Doncaster in December 1947, on the eve of railway nationalization.

which was to pull a train of up to 500 tons (508 tonnes) at express speeds, then requiring an average of between 60 and 65mph (97 and 105km/h), over long distances.

CHALK AND CHEESE

Even in the 1930s, 4-4-0s were still being built. The two types could hardly have been in greater contrast. The 'Dukedogs' of the GWR were built to cope with the light axle-loading requirements of the Cambrian lines; they used the outside frames of the obsolete 'Bulldog' class with a modern tapered Swindon boiler. With inside cylinders and outside cranks, they inevitably had an old-fashioned air. The 'Schools' class of the Southern, introduced by R.E.L. Maunsell in 1930, was also designed for a specific route, the tightly bending Hastings line, on which 4-6-0s were not allowed to run. With three cylinders, smoke deflectors and wide chimneys, they looked like express engines and performed similarly. Forty were built, and they ultimately ran on many routes apart from the Hastings one, often matching the performance of the 'Lord Nelsons'.

BELOW Originally No. 3283, this 'Duke' class 4-4-0 was built in 1897, re-boilered in 1905, and withdrawn in 1949. It was photographed at Aberystwyth in 1930.

2-8-2 P2 LNER 1934

Tractive effort: 44,000lb (19,955kg)

Axle load: 45,360lb (20.57 tonnes)

Cylinders: three 21x26in (533x660mm)

Driving wheels: 74in (188cm)

Heating surface: 3490sq ft (324.2m²)

Superheater: 635sq ft (59m²)

Steam pressure: 220psi (15.5kg/cm²)

Grate area: 50sq ft (4.6m²)

Fuel: Coal – 20,160lb (9.1 tonnes)

Water: 5000gall (6029 US) (22.75m³)

Total weight: 246,400lb (111.7 tonnes)

Overall length: 37ft 11in (11.58m)

One company was already operating Pacifics. The GNR had built its first Gresley 4-6-2 in 1922, just before the Grouping and also just before Sir Vincent Raven's 'City' class 4-6-2 for the North Eastern. The appointment of Gresley as first CME of the LNER confirmed that his design – which in any case was superior – would be the standard. In locomotive exchanges of 1925, however, the GW 'Castles' showed superior performance to the Gresley A1s, and Gresley and his team made a number of detailed modifications. By the time of the non-stop 'Flying Scotsman' of 1928, the A1s, some of them fitted with corridor tenders to enable a non-stop change of engine crew, were excellent performers. In 1928, Gresley also brought out his 'Super-Pacific', class A3, and these were doing first-rate service on the East Coast main line well before Stanier moved from Swindon to join the LMS in 1932 and set about providing the West Coast with a comparable stud of Pacifics.

The choice of Stanier was due not only to his abilities, but also to his Swindon training. The LMS's top brass had been greatly impressed by the power and economy of the GWR's *Launceston Castle* when it was borrowed for test purposes in 1928. Now Swindonian techniques and forms began to appear from the LMS works at Horwich, Crewe and Derby. Even before that, 1932 saw a widespread speeding-up of schedules and the introduction of new named trains such as the 'Liverpool Flyer' and 'Manchester Flyer' between these cities and Euston, hauled by 'Royal Scots'.

ABOVE Sir Nigel Gresley designed two 2-8-2 'Mikado' types for the LNER, the P1 goods engine of 1927 and the famous P2 express class, of which *Cock o' the North*, in 1934, was the first. This contemporary picture shows its original part-streamlined form. Later members of the class would be fully streamlined on the A4 model.

OPPOSITE TOP The zenith of LMS Pacific design was attained in the 'City' 4-6-2s. Here No 6254 *City of Stoke on Trent* passes Wavertree Junction, Liverpool, with a London express in the last years before nationalization. These engines had relatively small tenders, but operated over lines well supplied with water troughs.

FRENCH INSPIRATION

Just as De Glehn had given Churchward much food for thought in the 1900s, so another distinguished French engineer, André Chapelon, gave inspiration to Nigel Gresley in the early 1930s. Chapelon's speciality was the internal streamlining of locomotives to make steam flow with the minimum of restraint and the maximum of efficiency from boiler to cylinders. His work was influential in Gresley's design for the P2, Britain's only 2-8-2 'Mikado'-type express locomotives. The first of the six, *Cock o' the North*, appeared in 1934. With smaller driving wheels than the Pacifics (74in/187.9cm, compared to 80in/203.2cm), they were intended to operate on heavy Edinburgh–Aberdeen expresses; and with a tractive effort of more than 43,000lb (19,501kg), they were easily the most powerful passenger type produced in Britain. Although not built for high speed, they ran readily up to 85mph (137km/h).

The Pacifics were much faster. In March 1935, an LNER A3 Pacific, *Papyrus*, on a Newcastle–London test run, reached 108mph (174km/h), beating *City of Truro*'s 1904 record, but Gresley had more surprises in store. In

BELOW A preserved taper-boilered 0-6-0 GWR No 3205 at Llangollen, exactly the kind of line for which it was designed.

LEFT The LMS 4-cylinder 'Princess' class Pacific prototypes were built in 1932. A production batch, of which 46203 *Princess Margaret Rose* was one, followed in 1935, after some of the faults of the first models had been corrected. No 46203 is seen here at Kingmoor, Carlisle, on an up express.

OPPOSITE The appearance of the LNER 3-cylinder A4 Pacifics was a sensation in 1935. Later, the streamlined valances over the wheels and motion would be removed, but this illustration of No 4482 *Golden Eagle* shows the original appearance (*Mallard* is also restored to this form).

September of the same year, which marked 25 years of George V's reign, the LNER inaugurated a new express between London and Edinburgh, the 'Silver Jubilee', making the run in six hours. The world had not seen a train like this before. The loco-motive was a new 4-6-2 design, the A4. Though based on the well-proven A3, it looked strikingly different. It had a wedge-shaped front (which owed something to Gresley's friend Ettore Bugatti, the Italian racing car builder), a whaleback top, smoothed sides

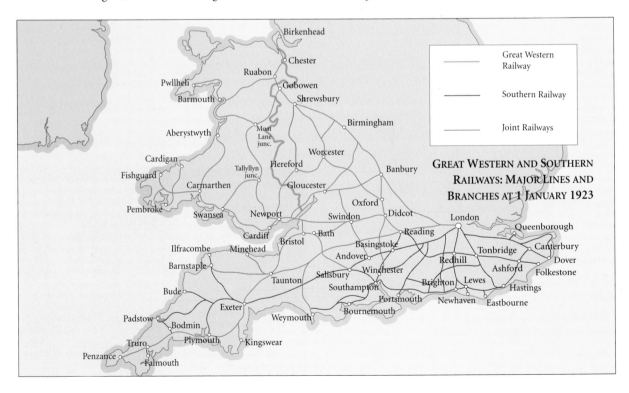

and a deep valance that covered much of the wheels and motion. The seven carriages were also streamlined. But the vital streamlining was in the steam passages concealed within the A4's silver-grey body. On the press run of the new train, the first of the class, *Silver Link,* ran from south of Hitchin to Holme, outside Huntingdon, at speeds consistently in excess of 100mph (161km/h), with a maximum of 112.5mph (181km/h).

On 3 June 1938, Gresley (by then Sir Nigel) used the excuse of some braking trials on the old Great Northern main line to find out just how fast one of his A4s could go. With a 240-ton (244-tonne) train and a steel-nerved King's Cross driver, John Duddingston, at the regulator, the answer, supplied by *Mallard,* was 126mph (203km/h). It was not achieved without damage to the engine: the middle cylinder big-end was broken. But *Mallard*'s record has never been surpassed by a steam locomotive.

The LMS, too, had its triumphs. Stanier had produced his first Pacific type, No 6200 *The Princess Royal,* in 1933. The two prototypes were carefully monitored, and a number of design changes, especially to the boiler, were made before others were built. The aim was to have an engine that could run on one tenderful of coal from London to Glasgow, and to make the outward and return trips, a total of 802.8 miles (1292km), within 24 hours. The 'Mid-day Scot' loaded up to 530 tons (538.5 tonnes), more than double the weight of the 'Silver Jubilee',

BELOW Class N on the LNER designated 0-6-2T, a large range, containing sub-types designed from the 1890s to the late 1930s. No 7999, an N7/4, seen here at Corfe Castle on the Swanage Railway, was built in 1924.

and had the summits of Shap and Beattock to climb. This was the true task and measure of the Stanier Pacifics, but the LMS also responded to the 'Silver Jubilee' with the 'Coronation Scot' of 1937, hauled by the 'Coronation' 4-6-2s, a streamlined development of the 'Princess Royal' class. On this train's trial run, 20 June 1937, No 6320 *Coronation* snatched the speed record with 114mph (183km/h), held until *Mallard*'s epic achievement a year later. The location of maximum speed – just two miles (3.2km) south of the facing cross-overs

at Crewe, where the train was due to stop – required very rapid braking. There was considerable relief among the engineers on board when it was safely accomplished.

ABOVE Gresley's second Pacific, the LNER A3 class of 1928, were known as the Super-Pacifics. Raised casings behind the chimney cover the superheater headers.

COMPETING GENIUSES

Enthusiasts still debate the respective merits of the Gresley and Stanier Pacifics (the latter's streamliners were later rebuilt as more conventionally shaped engines). Both chiefs produced one-off 'experimental' engines, with the LMS steam turbine Pacific proving more effective and durable in service than the LNER's 'hush-hush' 4-6-4 No 1000, of 1929, with a super-high-pressure boiler. Both also produced articulated Garratt-type locomotives for heavy mineral trains, Gresley's solitary 2-8-0+0-8-2 appearing in 1925, and Stanier's 2-6-0+0-6-2 class two years later (neither was a great success). In 1936, Gresley also produced the highly successful express freight V2 class 2-6-2, sometimes known as the 'Green Arrows': 184 were built, and they frequently appeared on passenger services. Gresley will remain most celebrated for his Pacifics and the Mikados.

LEFT Britain built Beyer-Garratt locomotives by the hundred for export, but only a small number ever ran on standard gauge here. The LNER had one; the LMS employed 33 on the Toton–Brent coal trains. Built between 1927 and 1933, they were not highly successful, partly because LMS engineers insisted on using standard parts not meant for articulated locomotives.

LEFT GWR 4-6-0 No 6990 *Witherslack Hall* approaches Quorn on the restored Great Central line. It is pulling a breakdown train, including a steam crane. The 'Hall' class, from 1928, was the GWR's standard mixed-traffic engine and the immediate ancestor of Stanier's LMS 'Black Five' of 1935.

BELOW Preserved A4 *Mallard* on the Scarborough Spa Express excursion train at York. On the side of the locomotive can be seen the plaque recording its achievement of the highest speed by a steam engine (won by a whisker from a German 4-6-4).

But Stanier's lasting achievement was with two more workaday types, a goods 2-8-0 and the celebrated 'Black Five', a mixed-traffic 4-6-0 which was built in large numbers (842 by 1949) and which, true to LMS philosophy, worked with equal effectiveness on freight or passenger trains over every part of the system. The 'Black Five' owed much to GW practice, particularly the GW 'Hall' class of 1928, which fulfilled a similar role on the Great Western. When war broke out in 1939 and the railways were once again put under extreme pressure, the Stanier 2-8-0 and 4-6-0 types proved invaluable.

4 · The Steam Railway at Work and at War

Reaching into every corner of the kingdom, the steam railway provides a remarkable range of services. And it responds superbly to the challenge of another global war.

LEFT Oil was second only to coal as a fuel for the railways. Not only a vital lubricant, right up to the end of the steam age, it also lit many stations and signal boxes, as well as the head- and tail-lights of trains and the vast majority of signal lights. Over the years, an immense range of oil lamps appeared, variations on a single theme.

OPPOSITE In the 1940s, the LMS developed a range of locomotive types, several of which became British Railways standard designs with only minor modifications. The Ivatt 2-6-0 light passenger engine, rated 2P, seen here at Kidderminster on the Severn Valley Railway, was one of these, intended for working branch line and local trains.

A GLANCE AT THE RAILWAY MAP OF BRITAIN in the 1930s, and even into the early 1960s, shows a network far greater in extent than the present-day one. Although uneconomic branch lines were closed every now and then, their total mileage was very small. Many were city railways, such as the Edinburgh–Leith or Nottingham suburban lines, killed off by trams and buses. The Big Four companies saw their rural lines as feeders to the main lines; they also inherited much of the attitudes of their predecessors, with a strong urge to defend their own territory. Country towns such as Cirencester, Lampeter, Crieff and Oakham took their place on the railway network for granted; many larger towns, such as Banbury, Bath, Wigan and Darlington, had two or more stations serving different lines. In 1914, Swansea had six stations belonging to five

LEFT Preserved Southern locomotives at work on a simulated 'Atlantic Coast Express'. 'King Arthur'-class 4-6-0 30777 *Sir Lamiel* and rebuilt 'West Country' 4-6-2 class 34039 *Boscastle* make a powerful double-header passing through the Great Central station at Quorn.

BELOW For a long time after the end of steam, this warning sign (now at Beamish Open Air Museum) still indicated an unguarded level crossing. The outline of a moving steam engine was unmistakable in a way that a diesel or electric locomotive could not be.

companies. The commuters of Windsor could take the GWR to Paddington or the LSWR to Waterloo. Numerous smaller places, such as Savernake in Wiltshire, also had two stations, where two lines crossed each other.

Some jointly operated big stations, such as Perth and Chester, offered alternative ways of travelling south. At Boat of Garten, a vastly smaller frontier station, a huge noticeboard was kept, suggesting to southbound passengers via the LMS Highland line that they would do better to take a (very slow) cross-country detour of about 90 miles (145km) and proceed south from Aberdeen via the LNER. Although no new lines were built, a number of important cut-offs were constructed, particularly on the Great Western, where bypass lines were built around Frome and Westbury to speed up express ser-vices between Reading and Taunton. Many junctions were improved, such as Rugby with its flyover where the Birmingham and Trent Valley routes diverge.

COMPLICATED PATTERNS

Cross-country lines traversed South-East and North Wales, enabling Birmingham–Hereford–Swansea and Chester–Pwllheli services to be run. Local lines linked East Anglian market towns such as Thetford and Bury St Edmunds. Very often, a cross-country working would shed and gather coaches at junctions, large or small. Tiny, peaceful places such as Halwill Junction in north Cornwall were enlivened daily by the arrival of the Atlantic Coast express, which, having shed coaches already at Exeter for Ilfracombe, was here divided into Bude and Padstow por-tions. In 1926, the Manchester–Bournemouth train, known as 'The Diner' to its staff (in the following year, it was formally named 'The Pines Express'), would leave Manchester at 10 a.m. with five coaches,

including a restaurant car, and pick up four more at Crewe from Liverpool. At Cheltenham, two of the four Liverpool coaches would be detached, to be connected to a Southampton-bound train following the route of the Midland and South Western Junction via Cirencester and Andover. In East Anglia, the 10.15 p.m. from Norwich to Liverpool Street was formed from the stock of three trains which had come from Yarmouth, Sheringham and Lowestoft. It ran via Wymondham to Ely, where it changed engines, then to Cambridge. Here two parcel vans were added before it left for London, arriving at 2.55 in the morning. Many trains followed more complicated patterns of addition and subtraction.

Certain lines, notably the Great Western, used 'slip coaches' on services to and from London. These specially fitted carriages could be automatically uncoupled from the train and, with a brakeman in charge, allowed to glide into the station, while the express sped on its non-stop way. Slip coaches were abandoned in the 1939–45 war, but the Western region of British Railways resuscitated them in 1950 and used them until 1960.

ABOVE The actual 'Cornish Riviera Express': 'King' class 4-6-0 No 6002 *King William IV* hammers through Reading (West) with the down train in summer 1938. It will work as far as Plymouth, where a 'Castle' will take over the train. 'Kings' were not allowed to cross the bridge at Saltash.

KING COAL

Coal was the mainstay of the steam railway in two ways, first as the fuel of the locomotives. The companies bought their coal as locally as possible to avoid the expense of running their own coal-supply trains. Seasoned travellers claimed to be able to tell the line by its smoke alone. The Great Western burned hard Welsh steam coal, and this was a helpful factor in the performance of its engines. Yorkshire coal was softer and flakier, more productive of smoke and soot, as travellers on the LNER lines might notice. The softest coal came from the Kent coalfield, and not the least of O.V.S. Bulleid's achievements was to fit his Pacifics with fireboxes that efficiently consumed the products of Betteshanger and Shepherdswell.

Coal also formed the principal bulk traffic. Where coalfields were, the density of railway lines increased. Most notably in South Wales, between Swansea and Newport, and in Yorkshire, between Doncaster and Barnsley, the railway geography was complicated in the extreme: each colliery was served by its own feeder line, and the narrow valleys were seamed with tracks at different levels. Coal was a major export, and the railway companies not only carried it to the sea, but also built, or inherited, dockyards

BELOW Re-enacting a once-typical dockland scene, preserved ex-LNER class Y7 0-4-0 'pug' No 68088, in British Railways livery, crosses the swing bridge at Boston Docks in November 2000. These tiny engines were vital for tightly curving dock and canalside lines.

4-4-0 SCHOOLS
SOUTHERN RAILWAY 1930

Tractive effort: 25,130lb (11,396kg)

Axle load: 23,520lb (10.6 tonnes)

Cylinders: three 16½x26in (419x660mm)

Driving wheels: 79in (200.5cm)

Heating surface: 1604sq ft (149m²)

Superheater: 280sq ft (26m²)

Steam pressure: 220psi (15.5kg/cm²)

Grate area: 28.3sq ft (2.6 m²)

Fuel: Coal – 11,200lb (5 tonnes)

Water: 4000gall (4804 US) (183m³)

Total weight: 150,080lb (68 tonnes)

Overall length: 25ft 6in (7.77m)

all round the coast. The LSWR had established Southampton as a major passenger port, and the Southern expanded the facilities with a fine new Ocean Terminal. The Great Western acquired the Barry Railway and its busy coal docks along with those of the Taff Vale at Cardiff. Across the Humber from Hull, the Great Central had established the coal port of Immingham (nowadays an importer of coal); the LNER profited from this, as it did from the dockyard lines set up by the NER and the Stockton & Darlington on Tyneside and on the Wear.

Heavy industry was still the backbone of the British economy. Above towns such as Coatbridge, Corby, Wrexham and Rotherham, the night sky was enflamed by furnaces; the 0-6-0Ts, the 0-8-0s and the 2-8-0s clanked in and out of works sidings, from yard to yard or city to city, with loose-coupled wagonloads, each train terminated by a brake van, with its ducket side window, wooden seat, brake wheel and the pipe from its coal-burning stove protruding from the roof.

SPECIALIZED VANS

The railways also carried a host of other items, some of them quite specialized. The LMS kept an elephant van at Rhyl for use in moving circuses around; it had special vans for theatre props, stabled at Oldham (Mumps) when not in use. The Southern had armoured bullion vans. Low-loader trucks were available for tall items. Perishable goods were dealt with urgently. Fish trains heading for Manchester and London, from Scotland, Fleetwood, Grimsby or Padstow, were given priority over passenger expresses. The driver of a train following behind had to

ABOVE The Southern Railway's three-cylinder 'Schools' class 4-4-0 of 1930 was the most up to date and powerful of its kind in Europe. Originally intended for the Hastings line, with its curves and gauge restrictions, it was so successful that the original 30 was increased to 40. They did express work on the Wessex route, as well as the Kent and Sussex lines.

BELOW Milk was a time-sensitive goods item, given priority treatment and transported by express trains. Milk churns could be seen at hundreds of country stations.

take extra care not to let his driving wheels slip on rails well-greased by fish oil and scales. When a banana ship arrived at Garston Dock, Liverpool, 10 trainloads of banana vans were mobilized to take the cargo. Special running conditions were observed to keep the fruit perfect: an even speed, no sudden halts, no jerking. Even more exotically, the Great Northern ran special trains in 1913 to convey up to 100,000 Sudanese quails at a time from Manchester Docks to London. Channel Island flowers were priority traffic to London from Weymouth. And one of the most familiar items

ABOVE J.M. Reid's imposing North British 4-4-2s dominated Scottish express services on the East coast from 1906 into the 1930s. Here, LNER No 9906 enters Carlisle with an express train off the Waverley Route from Edinburgh in 1934.

LEFT Locomotives for the Somerset & Dorset Railway were supplied by the Midland, one of the joint owners of the line. In this shot, two of the 2-8-0s, specially built from 1914 at Derby for this steeply graded line, stand awaiting duty at Bath Green Park shed.

on a country platform was a collection of milk churns. The Southern Railway alone owned a million of these, apart from milk tank wagons. Other liquids were carried: under the Midland's St Pancras terminus were great arched vaults where thousands of barrels of Burton beer were stored. Pigeon specials, pioneered by the North Eastern Railway, came to remote stations where the staff released the birds from racks of cages in special carriages to race back to their home lofts. Horseboxes were often seen attached to the rear of a country passenger train, a four-wheel van with a loose box and a tiny compartment for the groom.

A vast amount of parcel traffic was carried, in guards' vans and in special parcels trains between larger centres. Newspaper distribution was largely by train – for a long time the fastest train in the country was the little-known 2.32 a.m. Marylebone–Sheffield, which raced along the former Great Central metals at an average speed of over 60mph (97km/h), including stops. Usually hauled by an ex-GC locomotive, it consisted of one composite passenger coach and up to 10 newspaper vans. Virtually all mail went by train; while the Aberdeen and Penzance TPOs were the only exclusively postal trains, mailbags were as common a sight on platforms as milk churns (though more carefully watched), and a daily TPO carriage worked as far north as Helmsdale on the Highland line. At certain places on the lineside, mailbag pick-up posts were set, with the bags snatched up at speed by a net let out from one of the TPO vans.

The railways catered for a variety of seasonal and special traffic. Larger carriage depots kept rakes of superannuated coaches for use at certain peak times. In the

BELOW Road haulage services were biting heavily into the railway's freight traffic by the 1930s, and Sir Nigel Gresley's LNER class V2 3-cylinder 2-6-2 *Green Arrow* (named in connection with an express freight service), was designed as an answer, in 1936, to speeding up intercity goods trains.

LEFT The preserved LMS two-cylinder 2-8-0 No 48305 at Switherland, Great Central Railway. Introduced in 1935 as a mainline freight engine, in World War II, many were built for military use until the advent of the 'Austerity' 2-8-0.

OPPOSITE A 1950s sartorial study. Stationmaster Turrell at Euston wears a topper and tails, locomotive inspector Smith has a Homburg and brown coat, driver Gray wears a peaked cap and overalls, and fireman Moffat wears no hat (but presumably overalls). The engine is LMS Pacific 46240 *City of Coventry*.

BELOW The LNER class B1 4-6-0s were sometimes known as 'Antelopes', as a few had acquired zoological names including *Antelope* and *Springbok*. Most, like this anonymous example on a typical stopping-train duty, had no name.

northern industrial towns, all the factories took their holidays at the same time, and extra trains were required for the increase in traffic of 'Wakes Weeks', causing heavy congestion at such destination points as Blackpool, Skegness and Llandudno. The Southern kept what seemed specially disreputable carriages for the autumn hop pickers' trains from London into the Kentish countryside. Troop trains moved between army bases. In the 1920s, the little Derwent Valley line ran 'Blackberry Specials' from York in September for berry pickers. It was common practice up to the 1960s to hire a special train for events such as works outings and Sunday school picnic trips.

GOODS INCOME

For many country stations, it was goods rather than passenger traffic that brought revenue. Only the smallest did not possess a siding or two, a loading bank, a goods shed and a crane. Daily, or maybe only twice weekly, a local pick-up goods would come through, drawn by one of the ubiquitous 0-6-0s or sometimes by a pensioned-off passenger engine, such as the handsome LSWR T9 4-4-0s in the South West or their distant relations, the later versions of the Caledonian 'Dunalastairs', in Scotland. Both types lasted into the 1950s. The railway companies still had the obligation to be common carriers and accept whatever they could carry. In 1951, they still owned more than 7000 cart horses, used to deliver individual items on a local basis and sometimes also move wagons in the yards. The last railway horses were pensioned off in 1959.

4-6-2 MERCHANT NAVY SR 1943

Tractive effort: 38,000lb (17,233kg)
Axle load: 48,384lb (21.9 tonnes)
Cylinders: three 18x24in (457x609mm)
Driving wheels: 74in (188cm)
Heating surface: 2451sq ft (236m²)
Superheater: 822sq ft (76.3m²)
Steam pressure: 280psi (19.75kg/cm²)
Grate area: 48.5sq ft (4.5m²)
Fuel: Coal – 11,200lb (5.1 tonnes)
Water: 5000gall (6005 US) (22.75m³)
Total weight: 212,240lb (96.25 tonnes)
Overall length: 36ft 9in (11.2m)

Most British goods trains covered only a relatively short distance. Apart from a few city-to-city night express services, and specialized trains carrying fish or other perishable items, they were slow. Loose-coupled wagons meant that, at the top of any long, steep descent, the train had to stop while the guard went along unpinning the brakes on each wagon. At the foot, the opposite process had to be gone through. Wagons bound on a long cross-country journey were exchanged from train to train. Goods that were non-priority could take several days to reach their destination. Transfer goods engines exchanged wagons from one yard to another. A wagonload of slates from Llanberis (LMS) in Snowdonia, destined for a builder's yard in Lincoln, directly across the country, would be brought down the branch line to Caernarvon by a pick-up goods; attached to a Caernarvon–Chester goods that would stop at Menai Bridge to pick up any traffic from the Amlwch branch on Anglesey; re-attached to a Chester–Crewe train; shunted again at Crewe on to a Crewe–Derby

ABOVE The rebuilt 'Merchant Navy' Pacifics looked quite different (and were very different mechanically) to the original design, but remained imposing machines. Here No 35028 *Clan Line* transcends the unlovely surroundings of the coaling plant, as the fireman perches on the tender.

express goods via Burton on Trent; from Derby taken on a transfer working to Trent Yard; and finally attached to a Trent–Lincoln goods running via the old Midland line that still crosses the East Coast main line on the level at Newark, ending at the LMS goods yard in Lincoln – six different trains, though only one operating company. Although the system worked, it is possible to see why the single wagonload might be uneconomic for the railway and why, by the mid-1950s, the purchasers might send a lorry. In 1952, the railways possessed 956 marshalling yards, mostly of small size, in which goods trains were rearranged and assembled. By 1968, the last year of steam, the number had diminished to 184.

A MAJOR EMPLOYER

The railways were among the country's largest employers. In 1938, they employed more than 580,000 people, the great majority of them male; around three million of the population depended directly upon the railways. It was a man's world: apart from wartime emergency, women's posts were usually restricted to office work, cleaning and

ABOVE Pacifics returned to British rails in late 1922 when the Great Northern and North Eastern Railways both brought out 4-6-2 classes. The GN was first, with Gresley's A1 *Great Northern*, commemorating the company that was about to be merged into the LNER. The illustration shows the most famous of the class, No 4472 *Flying Scotsman*.

LEFT In the last years of steam, a grimy Class 5 4-6-0 hauls a long goods on the Midland main line. Introduced by the LMS in 1935, this two-cylinder mixed-traffic class, eventually more than 850-strong, did sterling service in every part of the country. For many, its sturdy looks typify the later British steam locomotive.

operating the gates at level crossings. Demarcation existed between the different departments of the civil engineer, the mechanical engineer, the loco-motive running superintendent and the traffic manager, though each offered a career path. A new recruit in the Running Department would start by cleaning engines and shovelling cinders, then become in sequence a fireman, a passed fireman with a driver's ticket and finally a driver. A few became inspectors and superintendents. In the station, a boy might start by filling oil lamps – still widely used through the system in the 1950s – and end up as a top-hatted station-master in a big terminus. The promotional

pyramid narrowed sharply, however, in the higher levels: most lamp boys, if they stayed on, would end their careers as signalmen or porters. In 1938, around 20,000 steam locomotives were in use, one for every 29 workers on the railway.

With the outbreak of war in 1939, once again state control was imposed. Once again, too, women played a larger part in railway operations, as signallers, clerks and ticket collectors. No woman ever drove a steam locomotive professionally – the task of a fire-man, the unavoidable preliminary to driving, was considered far too onerous. The fireman of a long-distance express had to shovel coal into the firebox at the rate of a ton an hour. Likewise, the task of a guard, or shunter, who required both muscle and expertise to operate the long-poled coupling hook which attached and detached wagons on the move, was an exclusively male preserve.

In World War II, the railways had the advantage of the large numbers of new loco-motives built in the 1930s, a far more standardized and efficient stud than that of 1914. They also had the asset of centralized traffic control. This had been pioneered by

ABOVE An interior shot of a locomotive roundhouse with engines grouped around the central turntable – Barrow Hill shed at Chesterfield is the only surviving working roundhouse in the country.

OPPOSITE Preserved LNER B1 4-6-0 No 61264 heads a Leicester train at Woodthorpe on the restored Great Central main line. The green livery harks back to a period in British Railways when the operating regions were allowed to apply their own colour schemes to passenger engines: in this case, London & North Eastern green.

LEFT A much-altered T9 4-4-0 of the LSWR, No 118, standing at Salisbury shed in 1933. The T9s were among Dugald Drummond's best and most-favoured designs. He would not have appreciated the altered smoke-box and the stovepipe chimney.

LEFT On the troughs: a 'Royal Scot' 4-6-0 in original form scoops up water at speed from Tebay troughs as it crosses the River Lune before climbing to Shap summit with the 'Royal Scot' London–Glasgow express. The sixth car is a clerestoried diner.

the Midland before World War I, with a control office at Derby monitoring and ordering train movements throughout the whole company system. Following the Grouping of 1923, this method was extended over the whole LMS network, with main regional centres at Crewe and Derby, and other district control offices as far north as Inverness. Each 'control' was in constant touch by telephone with train movements and events in its area, and the regional offices also kept a record of all locomotives and rolling stock, so that no piece of equipment was unaccounted for.

By 1939, all the Big Four had adopted the centralized control system. In wartime, it was even more vital and effective than in peacetime. Hour by hour, minute by minute, the effect of air raids could be minimized. Provision could be made for troop train

BELOW In the mid-1920s, a new batch of modified Great Central 'Director' 4-4-0s were built by the LNER for use on former North British lines. They were named after characters in Sir Walter Scott's novels. Here No 62674 *Flora MacIvor* pulls out of Melrose with a local train in April 1952.

4-6-0 5MT BLACK FIVE LMS 1934

Tractive effort: 26,000lb (11,790kg)
Axle load: 40,320lb (18.3 tonnes)
Cylinders: two 18½x28in (470x711mm)
Driving wheels: 72in (183cm)
Heating surface: 1460sq ft (135.6m²)
Superheater: 359sq ft (33.3m²)
Steam pressure: 225psi (15.8kg/cm²)
Grate area: 28.7sq ft (2.6m²)
Fuel: Coal – 20,160lb (9.1 tonnes)
Water: 4000gall (4804 US) (18m³)
Total weight: 159,040lb (72.1 tonnes)
Overall length: 27ft 2in (8.28m)

movements and for anti-aircraft gun patrols on the rails. Paths could be found for munitions trains. It was all the more necessary as air raids were now wreaking far more damage to the system than in the 1914–18 war. Many trains, particularly on the Southern, were shot up by fighter planes. The worst single effect of enemy bombing was not the destruction of engines (only eight were completely written off, with 484 damaged) or bridges, but the night when both the Manchester control office and its emergency replacement were destroyed. Operating a railway in blackout conditions created new problems, as well as hazards for staff working on platforms and in the yards. A steam locomotive working hard at night with a heavy load was hard to conceal – each time the fire door was opened a glare of red light rose up. And most engines had open cabs. Tarpaulins and blackout sheets were draped around, but drivers and firemen still had to be able to see out. Big stations had their glass roofs blackened over, and trains came and went in a twilight dimness.

ABOVE Some engines in the last production batches of LMS 'Class Fives', built after 1945, embodied experimental features. No 44687, photographed at Birmingham New Street, was fitted with Caprotti valve gear instead of the Walschaerts valve gear of the rest of the class, and also a double chimney and blast pipe.

STRATEGIC USE OF LINES

The way in which all main lines focused on London was a grave disadvantage to military traffic. As a result, certain lines not heavily used in peacetime became of great strategic importance. One was the now closed line from Didcot via Newbury to Winchester, where it joined the Waterloo–Southampton main line. It formed a vital north–south link for military traffic and was completely closed for public use for much of the war. In the run-up to D-Day, the invasion of Normandy in June 1944, the pressure on all lines in the South-East was intense. Those often forgotten but essential members of the railway world, the engineers who maintained the permanent way and its bridges, walls and other structures, coped daily with problems that would have been the stuff of nightmares up to 1940.

Inevitably, during six years of maximum strain and effort, the railways gradually became run-down and decrepit. Restaurant cars and sleepers were dropped for the duration of the war, but once again, free buffets for troops in transit appeared at all

LEFT In 1943, the Ministry of Supply ordered the 'Austerity' 9F 2-8-0, based to a large extent on parts available from the LMS 8F. The requirement was for a simple two-cylinder engine that was easily maintained and could deliver a high tractive effort. No 77081 was fitted with a vacuum brake pump for heavy mineral trains.

BELOW LNER 4-6-4 No 10000. This was Britain's sole specimen of the 'Hudson' type, so popular in the USA and Canada. Built in 1929 with an experimental high-pressure boiler, it was rebuilt in 1937 with the same boiler as the A4 Pacifics, which it closely resembled. It kept its unique extra trailing wheels.

major stations. 'Is your journey really necessary?' asked disapproving posters; however, with their frequency much reduced, long-distance trains were often heavily overloaded: 20-coach trains out of King's Cross and Euston were by no means unusual. Travel by train in wartime was rarely a pleasant experience, and the railways suffered in public perception for difficulties and delays for which they could not be responsible.

Although once again railway workshops, both company and private, had turned out tanks, armoured cars, guns and other war items, locomotive building was not neglected. Stanier's LMS 2-8-0 and 4-6-0 types, both versatile engines, were built for use on other lines as well. In 1942, a coopted team of designers developed the 'Austerity' 2-8-0 and 2-10-0 types, constructed for the Ministry of Supply and used by the War Department to haul military freight. Pared of all inessential features and with working parts made as accessible as possible, these locomotives had a somewhat gaunt appearance compared to the conventional British engine. They did a first-rate job, however, and were very popular with engine crews. Many hundreds were built and shipped overseas, as well as used at home.

4-6-2 DUCHESS LMS 1938	
Tractive effort: 40,000lb (18,140kg)	
Axle load: 49,952lb (22.6 tonnes)	
Cylinders: four 16½x28in (419x711mm)	
Driving wheels: 81in (205.75cm)	
Heating surface: 2807sq ft (260m²)	
Superheater: 856sq ft (79.5m²)	
Steam pressure: 250psi (17.6kg/cm²)	
Grate area: 50sq ft (4.6m²)	
Fuel: Coal – 22,400lb (10.1 tonnes)	
Water: 4000gall (4804 US) (18m³)	
Total weight: 235,200lb (106.6 tonnes)	
Overall length: 37ft (11.28m)	

ABOVE One of the features of the LMS 'Duchess' 4-6-2s was a steam-powered coal pusher in the tender, which brought the coal forwards to the fireman, a valuable aid on a long haul, such as the 290 miles (466km) between Crewe and Perth with the Inverness-bound 'Royal Highlander' sleeper train.

REMARKABLE DESIGNS

On the Southern, under an enterprising and original-minded CME, Oliver Bulleid, a new three-cylinder Pacific type emerged in 1941. To avoid accusations of waste in constructing a new express passenger locomotive in the middle of a world war, it was officially classed as mixed-traffic. Bulleid had been one of Gresley's assistants, but his engines owed little to the Doncaster tradition. The boiler, with a pressure of 280lb (127kg), was hidden beneath an almost straight-sided 'air-smoothed' casing; it had solid American-style 'Boxpok' wheels and internal valve gear, chain-driven through a lubricating oil bath. It was packed with original features. There were two variants: the 'Merchant Navy' class and the lighter 'West Country' class. Pacifics, with their longer wheelbase and greater axle weight, were usually confined to mainline working, but the 'West Country' class could run over 90 per cent of the Southern's network.

Bulleid also designed the remarkable Q1 0-6-0 for mixed-traffic work, built to 'Austerity' standard without a running board; its resemblance to a giant clockwork toy prompted Sir William Stanier to ask its designer: 'Where's the key?' But the Q1, the most powerful 0-6-0 built in Britain, proved a most useful engine. Unlike most tender engines, it could go as well in reverse as in forward gear; running tender-first, it achieved a speed of 75mph (120km/h), allegedly with Bulleid sitting on the buffer beam.

LEFT Ex-LNER A1 4-6-2 60161 *North British* leaves Edinburgh Waverley with the southbound 'Queen of Scots' Pullman. Designed by A.H. Peppercorn and built in 1948, this was a modern locomotive despite its traditional Gresleyan appearance, and it gave excellent service until dieselization brought about its premature end. The last was retired in July 1966.

5 • The Last Years of Steam

After achieving triumphs of speed and contributing admirably to the war effort, the steam locomotive enters decline in the second half of the twentieth century. Political changes bring an end to the Big Four, while economic and environmental concerns prompt the swift abandonment of steam traction.

LEFT Night train scene on the Gloucestershire & Warwickshire Railway: the tank engine and its one-coach train wait at the empty platform of a country station. Re-enacted for 'atmosphere', this was the actual state of things all too often in the last years of steam traction.

OPPOSITE Preserved British Railways standard 4MT 2-6-4T No 80104 drains off the cylinder cocks as it begins to reverse into the station at Swanage. Its descent from the LMS 2-6-4 type is clear, but the design is more fluid – and it is a two-cylinder engine. Built in 1955, it is one of Britain's last production steam locomotives.

THE POSTWAR GENERAL ELECTION of 1945 brought in a Labour government, part of the programme of which was to bring the country's railways under state ownership. The Transport Act of 1947 set up a central Railway Executive, and the nationalized system took effect from 1 January 1948. The Big Four companies were replaced by six regions: Eastern, London Midland, North Eastern, Western, Scottish and Southern.

Despite their imminent demise, the old companies did not wholly mark time. The Southern continued to expand the stud of 'Merchant Navy' Pacifics and their lighter companions, now also known as the 'Battle of Britain' class and named after RAF squadrons, rather than West Country towns. Bulleid also built an experimental locomotive which he hoped would rival the performance of the new diesel-electric engines being tested by the LMS; however, his bogie-mounted 'Leader' never got past the pro-totype stage. The LMS, at which H.G. Ivatt had succeeded Sir William Stanier, was rebuilding the 'Royal Scots' and their lighter counterparts, the 'Patriots', and greatly improving their performance; 'Black Fives', sometimes with experimental modifica-tions such as Caprotti valve gear, continued to appear.

There were controversial developments on the LNER. During the war, Gresley's suc-cessor, Edward Thompson, had rebuilt the P2 2-8-2s as rather ungainly-looking 4-6-2s, classed A2/2, to a howl of protest from Gresley's admirers. Thompson, however, was a standardization man. He provided the LNER with a much-needed good 'utility' 4-6-0, the B1 class, using the 'Sandringham'-class boiler, the K2-class cylinders and other standard parts, so avoiding the costs of new patterns and tools. He went on to produce a new Pacific, the three-cylinder A2/1, in 1944. Further acrimony was kindled by his drastic rebuild of the very first Gresley Pacific, *Great Northern*. Rightly or wrongly, it was seen as a deliberate slur on his distinguished predecessor. Just before his retirement in 1946, Thompson brought out his most successful Pacific design, classed A2/3. Fifteen were built.

His successor, A.H. Peppercorn, produced a further two Pacific designs. The first was classed as A2 (former classification of the by now scrapped Raven Pacifics) and 64 were built, nearly all of them under the nationalized British Railways. His A1 followed

OPPOSITE A GWR 'King' 4-6-0 class on the 'Cornish Riviera Express' emerges at speed from the tunnel at Horse Cove, where the Exeter–Plymouth line hugs the coast. The '130' on the smoke-box door is the train's identifying number.

BELOW The LNER Pacifics were often seen on secondary services as dieselization progressed in the early 1960s. Edward Thompson's A2 60520 *Watling Street* is seen here on a parcels train.

in mid-1948, and 49 of these were built. The reclassification of LNER Pacifics in the 1940s can be confusing. The rebuilt *Great Northern* was reclassified first as A1 and later as A1/1. Including rebuilds, the LNER managed to produce six Pacific designs between 1943 and 1948, adding to the four bequeathed by Gresley, whose A1s became A10s.

HIGH ENGINEERING STANDARDS

The company that showed the least degree of innovation was the Great Western. 'Kings' and 'Castles' still ran its express services, but they were acquiring a rather old-fashioned air. The Churchward-Collett tradition remained very much in force. F.W. Hawksworth succeeded the latter in 1941 and produced the two-cylinder 'County' 4-6-0 in 1945, the ultimate descendant of the 'Saints'. Like the 'Merchant Navy' class, it was rated as a mixed-traffic engine, with 75in (190.5cm) coupled wheels, though the intention was for express passenger work. The GWR was still building 0-6-0 pannier tanks, little different from those of earlier generations, in 1948.

What Swindon did have, and other centres lacked (until the establishment of the Locomotive Testing Plant at Rugby in 1948), was a testing plant where the performance of an engine could be assessed in the workshops. GW engineering was still working to a higher standard of precision than any other company's.

BELOW The rebuilt and preserved Southern Railway 'West Country' 4-6-2 34039 *Boscastle* bears the nameplate of the 'Atlantic Coast Express', which it might well have hauled in regular service. Here it is on an exhibition run.

LEFT Channel Island steamers at Weymouth berthed alongside the harbour station; a tank engine drew the train, at walking pace, along the pier to join the main line, where more substantial motive power was waiting to make the swift run to London.

OPPOSITE British Railways standard 'Britannia' class 4-6-2 70032 *Tennyson* with an Eastern Region Norwich express. Fifty-five of this class were built between 1951 and 1953. Their impact on the London–Norwich service was dramatic, with a 20 per cent improvement on the previous best timings.

When it became the Western Region, though, it was a Darlington-trained mechanical engineer, Alfred Smeddle, who took over at Swindon; he completely regenerated the 'Kings' by fitting them with double blast-pipe chimneys and a number of other modifications which gave them a new lease of life as high-performance engines. Reciprocally, a Swindon man, K.J. Cook, went to Doncaster on Peppercorn's retirement and introduced a degree of fine tuning with optical instruments that markedly improved performance.

But the Railway Executive, whose locomotive specialist member was R.A. Riddles, a former senior LMS engineer, was pressing towards a single national standard of locomotive design, with a set of basic types which should fulfil all service needs.

RIGHT The ill-assorted protuberances on the boiler top, the high running plate, tall chimney and boxy tender combine to give the LMS Ivatt 2-6-0 a somewhat foreign look. American and Continental influences are visible in the design. All too often in the past, however, British designers had been too insular in their attitudes.

Particularly on the Southern, a great deal of electrification had taken place using the third-rail system, and the heavily used Sheffield–Manchester freight route via the Woodhead Tunnel was being equipped with overhead electrification, completed in 1954. At this time, though, it was hardly questioned that steam should continue to be the principal source of motive power.

There were historic and economic reasons for this. Railways and the coal industry had been intimately linked for 150 years. The mines, also brought into public ownership in 1948, were the railways' biggest customer; the railways were the mines' third-largest customer, after the gas and electricity industries. In the immediate postwar years, as a peacetime economy struggled to become established, there was no capital available for large-scale conversion to electrified traction (something that had been contemplated for the East Coast main line since the 1930s). It was easiest to press on with coal-fired steam traction in its most efficient forms.

BELOW The most successful of all the BR standard types designed under the auspices of R.A. Riddles was the 9F 2-10-0. In this 1965 photograph, No 92234 heads south over Rowington troughs on a Birmingham Washwood Heath–Eastleigh vacuum-brake fitted freight. To the right of the engine is the troughs' water tank.

4-6-2 BRITANNIA BR 1951

Tractive effort: 32,000lb (14,512kg)

Axle load: 46,144lb (20.9 tonnes)

Cylinders: two 20x28in (508x711mm)

Driving wheels: 74in (188cm)

Heating surface: 1950sq ft (181.2m²)

Superheater: 530.6sq ft (49.2m²)

Steam pressure: 250psi (17.6kg/cm²)

Grate area: 42sq ft (3.9m²)

Fuel: Coal – 15,680lb (7.1 tonnes)

Water: 4200gall (5044 US) (19m³)

Total weight: 210,560lb (95.5 tonnes)

Overall length: 36ft 6in (11.12m)

Many observers felt that such forms already existed among the more recent locomotive types inherited by British Railways. There were plenty to choose from. The rebuilt 'Merchant Navy' and 'West Country' Pacifics of the Southern were reliable and powerful, apart from a propensity to wheel-slipping. In the inter-regional locomotive tests of 1948, a 'West Country' put in some remarkable work on the Highland main line between Perth and Inverness. The Peppercorn A1 Pacifics scored very high for reliability, although they could be rough riders (in an average lifetime of about 15 years, the class members fitted with roller bearings ran over a million miles [1,609,300km] apiece). The LMS 'Black Five' was an established staple. The GW 'Kings', fitted with double-blast chimneys from 1953, excelled even on their previous merits. And in fact all these types, and very many more, survived in service until the end of the steam era (it was assumed that the useful life of a locomotive was anywhere from 30 to 50 years). Perhaps it was such variety, combined with the jealous, old-established company loyalties behind each, that made Riddles and his team opt for a completely new set.

ABOVE In line with official philosophy, the 'Britannias' were two-cylinder, simple-expansion engines, free of gadgetry and intended to be easy to drive and maintain, with the working parts as get-at-able as possible. No 70013 *Oliver Cromwell* is shown on the traverser at Crewe works, in 1967, when it was the last steam engine to be repaired there for British Railways.

NEW-LOOK ENGINES

The new engines, sharing a distinct family look, began to be unveiled from 1951 onwards, starting with a new Pacific, the 'Britannia', classed as 7MT and intended for fast freight as well as passenger duties. It was followed by two 4-6-0 mixed-traffic types, 5MT and 4MT (one with a lighter axle-loading than the other), and two tank types, a 2-6-4T classed as 4P and a 2-6-2T classed as 3P. Later, three types of 2-6-0 and a lightweight 2-6-2T were also added to the range. A lighter Pacific, the 6P 'Clan', was built in small numbers. The final product was a 9F 2-10-0 goods engine. Surprisingly perhaps, there

2-6-4T BRITISH RAILWAYS 1951

Tractive effort: 25,500lb (11,564kg)

Axle load: 43,792lb (19.8 tonnes)

Cylinders: two 18x28in (457x711mm)

Driving wheels: 68in (17.75cm)

Heating surface: 1366sq ft (126.9m²)

Superheater: 245sq ft (22.7m²)

Steam pressure: 225psi (15.8kg/cm²)

Grate area: 26.7sq ft (2.5m²)

Fuel: Coal – 7840lb (3.5 tonnes)

Water: 2000gall (2400 US) (9m³)

Total weight: 194,880lb (88.4 tonnes)

Overall length: 38ft 6in (11.74m)

was no 2-8-0 among the standard types: this wheel arrangement had been the principal mainline freight engine of all of the Big Four. But more than 700 of the 'Austerity' 2-8-0s were in service.

The BR 'standards' attracted mixed opinions on all counts. Their design was intended to make maintenance as straightforward as possible, and the high running-plates and exposed piping offended some purists. In service, they did not exceed the performance of comparable types, and the 'Britannias' were criticized by enginemen for hot, noisy cabs compared with the Gresley and Stanier Pacifics. The 'Clans' were undistinguished in performance. The 4-6-0 was hardly more than a revamp of the 'Black Five'. A single prototype of an express passenger type, rated 8P, No 71000 *Duke of Gloucester*, was built. Unfortunately it proved to have serious problems with its boiler and consequently was little used. Rescued from scrap in 1973 and extensively rebuilt, its restored form suggests that the type could have been a true Super-Pacific.

The undoubted star of the BR range was the 2-10-0, which proved capable of very fast running – up to 90mph (145km/h) at least – and it was used on summer passenger trains on the hilly Somerset & Dorset line. In Britain, high speed had always been identified with big driving wheels, a legacy of the old nineteenth-century single-drivers; however, the 9F's coupled wheels were only 60in (152cm) in diameter. Some were built

ABOVE The finely drawn lines of the BR standard 2-6-4T 80098, picked out by the paint lining of tanks and bunker, are apparent in this view, as it approaches Swanwick station, at the Midland Railway Centre.

OPPOSITE The scene at Ropley shed on the Mid-Hants railway, in 1997, conveys something of the old-time steam depot, although the traditional architecture of sooty brick and arched doorways and windows is lacking. The engines on shed are appropriately of Southern Railway origin, although mostly in BR livery.

with a Crosti boiler, intended to preheat the water and so speed up steam production. It was suggested that they could be used to haul expresses on the Highland main line (train-heating equipment would have had to be installed), but this never happened.

Standardization was embarked upon in other ways too. New standard coaching stock was introduced from 1951, and the problem of standardizing and modernizing a vast range of different wagon types was beginning to be tackled.

From 1952 onwards, however, the shades began to close in on the steam-powered railway. In the postwar world of light industry and 'clean' power, the steam locomotive began to seem a smoky relic of a bygone time. It was more and more difficult to find staff prepared to undertake the gruelling task of the fireman and the grubby job of the engine cleaner. A society increasingly sensitive to pollution looked askance at the pall of smoke that hung over any large locomotive depot. The national railway system, still employing nearly 600,000 people, was losing money. The 1947 Transport Act had envisaged a coordinated national policy for inland transport, with rail, canal and road all combined in an integrated system. Political changes in the 1950s, allowing 'free enterprise' on the roads, put a stop to that, and soon road haulage was carrying more freight than the railways. The need for economy and cost-saving resulted in lower standards of maintenance and cleanliness.

ABOVE In 1948, F.W. Hawksworth produced a new variant on the 0-6-0T theme for the Western Region of BR, in this powerful side-tank engine with outside cylinders and Walschaerts valve gear. No 1501 of the class is seen here at Kidderminster on the Severn Valley Railway.

EFFECTS OF MODERNIZATION

In January 1955, a new modernization plan for the railways was unveiled by Sir Brian Robertson, chairman of the British Transport Commission. An investment of £1200 million was to be made in new facilities. 'Modernization' became the key word of railway managers, and modernization meant, above all, two things. One was a much reduced network. The other was the abandonment of steam traction. The plan noted that 'many factors combine to indicate that the end of the steam era is at hand. These include the growing shortage of large coal suitable for locomotives; the insistent demand for a reduction in air pollution by locomotives and far greater cleanliness in trains and railway stations; and the need for better acceleration.'

Riddles was not wedded to steam, but considered that, in the conditions of the time, it provided 'the most tractive effort per pound sterling'; he had been building new steam locomotives with the expectation of their lasting until large-scale electrification took place, a period of perhaps 20 years. The policy of general introduction of diesel-powered

2-8-0 8F LMS 1935

Tractive effort: 33,000lb (14,965kg)
Axle load: 34,720lb (15.75 tonnes)
Cylinders: two 18½x28in (470x711mm)
Driving wheels: 56½in (143.5cm)
Heating surface: 1463sq ft (136m²)
Superheater: 235.25sq ft (21.8m²)
Steam pressure: 225psi (15.8kg/cm²)
Grate area: 28.7sq ft (2.6m²)
Fuel: Coal – 20,160lb (9.1 tonnes)
Water: 4000gall (4804 US) (18m³)
Total weight: 159,040lb (72.1 tonnes)
Overall length: 26ft (7.93m)

OPPOSITE Prestige trains of the 1950s: LNER class A4 4-6-2 60032 *Seagull* leaves Kings Cross and approaches Copenhagen Tunnel with the down 'Tees-Tyne Pullman', while A3 60044 *Melton* backs towards the terminus to attach the 'Yorkshire Pullman', the nameplate already fitted above the smoke-box door.

BELOW An LMS 8F 2-8-0, No 48399, approaches the highest station in England, Dent on the Settle–Carlisle line, with a lengthy mixed goods.

engines immediately altered that. This sentence of death for steam locomotives, even if set for the future, had an immediate impact. Care and maintenance could not be entirely stopped, as the traffic schedules had to be maintained, but a run-down in standards began and became progressively more noticeable. Research and development came to a halt. As more and more diesel multiple-unit trains and diesel-electric locomotives appeared, so the declining stock of steam engines became ever more grimy, decrepit and unreliable.

There were a few exceptions to this. Gresley's A4s, finally displaced from the East Coast main line, spent a few years from 1960 to 1964 hauling fast, lightweight Edinburgh–Aberdeen expresses, cherished by Haymarket Shed in Edinburgh just as when they had been the pride of British land transport.

THE END IN SIGHT

In the last years of steam, there were occasional moments when drivers, often with their own retirement at hand, and perhaps more aware than anyone of the approaching end of an era, allowed themselves a 'last fling' when the locomotive was up to it. On one of those occasions, in 1964, a rebuilt

BELOW The Bulleid 'West Country' class Pacific 21C23, in original Southern malachite green paintwork.

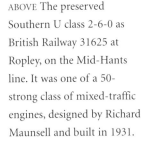

'Merchant Navy', 35005, topped 100mph (161km/h) between Basingstoke and Winchester on the 21.20 Waterloo–Southampton. On a similar occasion, the double-chimneyed *King Richard III* reached 102mph (164km/h) while hauling the down 'Bristolian'. Such feats were often encouraged by amateur enthusiasts, keen to log a performance never likely to be repeated.

In 1962, the railways were finally relieved of their responsibility as a common carrier to accept any freight. The number of goods trains and depots fell drastically and with

ABOVE The preserved Southern U class 2-6-0 as British Railway 31625 at Ropley, on the Mid-Hants line. It was one of a 50-strong class of mixed-traffic engines, designed by Richard Maunsell and built in 1931.

LEFT The non-stop King's Cross–Edinburgh 'Elizabethan' passes Welwyn Garden City in 1956, hauled by one of the last LNER A4 4-6-2s, 60007 *Sir Nigel Gresley*, named after its designer. Engines for the non-stop service were fitted with corridor tenders to allow a change of engine crew.

it the number of goods locomotives. The reduction in the steam stud was further accelerated from 1964 by the implementation of the 1963 Beeching Report, 'The Reshaping of British Railways'. The consequent closure of many branch and secondary main lines – and of some main lines, such as Dumfries–Stranraer, that might have been regarded as of strategic importance – sent thousands of locomotives to the scrap-yards. As electrification and dieselization proceeded, the territory occupied by steam locomotives grew smaller. A yellow stripe across the cabside number indicated 'Not to Work South of Crewe'. Passengers became familiar with long lines of condemned engines standing at former locomotive depots. Barry Island, in South Wales, was the largest but by no means the only engine-breaking yard.

In these latter years, only the 9F 2-10-0 remained in production. One of these, 92250, was the last steam engine to be built at Crewe Works, in 1958. The very last, No 92220, was completed at Swindon in March 1960, and, uniquely in the class, given a name – *Evening Star*.

In 1952, British Railways had 19,276 route miles (31,021km), 8212 stations (passenger or goods) and 956 marshalling yards (mostly small). In 1968, the last year of steam traction, the route mileage of British Rail (renamed thus in 1964) was 12,447 (20,031km), the number of stations and depots was 3155 and the number of marshalling yards was 184. Over the same 16-year period, 20,000 steam locomotives, many of them with up to 30 years of potential active life ahead of them, were scrapped. As the last representatives of famous locomotive types were withdrawn, the call for preservation of at least one example was invariably made, although not always successfully.

BELOW The preserved A4 60009 *Union of South Africa* is one of the members of the class fitted with a double chimney and blast pipe, which improved an already exceptional performance. The characteristic chime whistle of the A4 can be seen in front of the chimney.

6 • Little Lines

At the end of the steam era, a wonderful, and sometimes weird, collection of minor lines could be found across the country, often preserving antique equipment. Run and lovingly maintained by dedicated enthusiasts, a surprising number of them still exist today, introducing a whole new generation to the joys of steam.

LEFT Engines often did seem to spend a certain amount of time standing around doing nothing …

OPPOSITE One of 15 preserved LMS 'Black Fives', No 45248 brings a passenger train round a curve on the Keighley and Worth Valley Railway. This was by far the most widely distributed locomotive class. It was stationed throughout the system, from Wick to Bournemouth, undertaking every kind of work from fast passenger trains to local goods services.

SOME EUROPEAN COUNTRIES developed a cross-country network of light railways, mostly narrow-gauge, complementary to both the mainline system and its secondary cross-country lines. This never happened in England or Scotland. The Light Railways Act of 1896 was designed to encourage the building of rural lines to an easier specification than main lines and did result in the building of numerous standard-gauge branches, although most of the lines built under the Act were short-lived. They were normally operated by the 'one engine in steam' principle, which meant that only one engine ran on the line, simplifying operations considerably. Goods and passengers were usually conveyed in one mixed train.

In the years before 1914, there emerged the distinctive figure of Colonel Holman Fred Stephens, a determined advocate of light railways, who assembled under his ownership or management an amazingly varied set of lines. The largest unit was the Kent & East Sussex Railway, but he also had the East Kent, the Weston, Clevedon & Portishead, and the Shropshire & Montgomery railways. Stephens brought the latter back from the dead, but his lines rarely paid their way. They became famous for the antique and heterogeneous locomotives and rolling stock likely to be found on them, referred to by one writer as 'an animated railway museum'. Although the K&ESR was

ABOVE Preserved ex-LMS 2-6-4T, British Railways 42085, running in sylvan surroundings on the Lakeside & Haverthwaite railway in Cumbria. This type of engine was built for heavy passenger suburban services, and there were several LMS classes from around 1930. This one, designed by C.E. Fairburn, was built in 1951.

LEFT Locomotive No 4 of the Talyllyn Railway, the 0-4-2 saddle-tank *Edward Thomas*, nearing Rhydronen on the downhill run from Abergynolwyn to Towyn. Built originally for the closed Corris Railway, it was acquired by Talyllyn in 1951.

run with relatively up-to-date stock, at the Shropshire & Montgomery's little depot at Kinnerley Junction he had such items as a Bury engine, *Severn*, dating back to 1840, and a tiny 0-4-2T, *Gazelle*, coupled to a former horse-drawn tramcar of the London County Council. Also in use was the ex-LSWR Royal saloon of 1844, as the Colonel's inspection vehicle.

Colonel Stephens was also involved, at different times, with various narrow-gauge lines. Narrow-gauge lines were rare in England. The Light Railways Act had prompted the building of two, the 2ft 6in (76.2cm) gauge Leek & Manifold line in North Staffordshire, which ran between 1904 and 1934, and the 23½in (60cm) Lynton & Barnstaple, in North Devon (1898–1935). Among the few other English narrow-gauge lines were the Southwold Railway in East Anglia (3ft/91.4cm gauge), linking the town to the GER at Halesworth, and closing down in 1929; and the 23½in (60cm) Ashover Railway in Derbyshire, built as a stone carrier, but, under Colonel Stephens's aegis, also running passenger services from 1924 to 1931. The latter closed completely in 1950. The Ravenglass & Eskdale Railway was originally a narrow-gauge minerals-hauling line, which closed in 1913 and reopened in 1915, rebuilt to a miniature gauge for visitor traffic. Also on a miniature gauge (15in/38cm) is the Romney Hythe &

BELOW There is no mistaking a steam locomotive's departure. A whistle blows hoarsely. Steam hisses forth, smoke rises and a determined noise, slow at first but rapidly increasing in frequency, can be heard. On the Swanage Railway, BR standard 2-6-4T 80104 shows it all on leaving the terminus with an empty stock train for Norden.

Dymchurch Railway in Kent. Although built in 1926 as its rich owners' toy and a tourist attraction rather than as a serious railway, it performed useful service in World War II as a military supply line, with a unique miniature armoured train.

Scotland had only one steam-worked narrow-gauge railway, the 2ft 6in (76.2cm) Campbeltown & Machrihanish, running across the southern tip of the Kintyre Peninsula. Built after the Light Railways Act of 1906, and far from any other railway line, it lasted until 1932.

WELSH NARROW GAUGE

In Wales, numerous narrow-gauge railways were built. Some of them, indeed, pre-dated steam and the standard gauge, using pony haulage. The usual reason for choosing narrow gauge was difficult terrain, and the usual reason for building such a line was the transport of mineral or stone traffic. Such lines were especially numerous in the mountain-ous districts of Wales. East and west of the Snowdon massif, several railways clung to, and tunnelled through,

ABOVE This scene of slate quarry working demonstrates what lines such as the Ffestiniog and Talyllyn were all about, in the days when Wales exported thousands of tons of quarried and cut slate. Most of it was sent down to the coast by narrow-gauge railway, for onward shipment by sea.

LEFT Peckett 0-4-2 side-tank engine Karen, photographed on the Welsh Highland Railway. It was built in 1942 to haul chrome ore at the Selukwe Park Light Railway in Rhodesia (now Zimbabwe). Brought back to Britain in 1976, it was restored by 1983.

the mountainsides, in order to serve the vast slate quarries which were at a peak of activity between 1860 and 1903.

The oldest of these was the Ffestiniog Railway, established in 1836, though it did not acquire steam engines until 1863. Many pundits prophesied that its 23½in (60cm) gauge was too narrow to support a steam locomotive. The Ffestiniog triumphantly proved them wrong with its first engine, *Little Wonder*, a highly original double-ended locomotive designed by Robert Fairlie, effectively two boilers mounted on a single frame, each resting on a four-wheel bogie driven by outside cylinders, with a central firebox and cab. The Ffestiniog ran passenger services from 1865 and was the first British line to use an eight-wheel bogie carriage. Its inland terminal, the slate-mining town of Blaenau Ffestiniog, was also later tapped by two long standard-gauge branches, one from the LNWR main line at Llandudno Junction, the other from the Cambrian's cross-country line at Bala. Hit by the decline in slate usage, the Depression and World War II, the Ffestiniog line closed for passengers in September 1939, and for goods traffic in 1946. Since 1955, happily, it has been revived and restored by voluntary work and contributions.

To the west, the North Wales Narrow Gauge (later the Welsh Highland) opened in 1877, from Dinas Junction on the LNWR's Caernarvon–Afon Wen line, to Quellyn Lake and later to Beddgelert. It went into receivership in 1878, and its existence always remained precarious. Nevertheless, it completed the line from Beddgelert to Porthmadog in 1923, connecting with the Ffestiniog and forming with it the longest narrow-gauge line in Britain, at 34 miles (55km). The two lines were worked as one, under the management of the ubiquitous Colonel Stephens, until the Welsh Highland's closure in 1937.

BELOW A Fairlie 'double-engine' from the Ffestiniog Railway, 0-4-4-0 Earl of Merioneth, earlier called Taliesin, and built at the line's own works in 1885. Another of the three Ffestiniog Fairlies was built in 1979, based on patents going back to 1864 for a 'double-bogie articulated locomotive'.

0-4-4-0 FAIRLIE FFESTINIOG RLY 1872

Tractive effort: 7500lb (3400kg)
Axle load: 5600lb (2.54 tonnes)
Cylinders: four 8½x14in (216x355mm)
Driving wheels: 32in (81.25cm)
Heating surface: 713sq ft (66.2m²)
Superheater: n/a
Steam pressure: 140psi (9.9kg/cm²)
Grate area: 11.2sq ft (1m²)
Fuel: Coal – 11,200lb (5 tonnes)
Water: 720gall (864 US) (3.3m³)
Total weight: 44,912lb (20.4 tonnes)
Overall length: 18ft 8in (5.69m)

ABOVE The miniature gauge Ravenglass & Eskdale Railway has turntables at its termini, in order to have its loco-motives working forwards. At first glance, this looks like a scene from a railway of much greater gauge.

Further south, the Corris Railway, of 2ft 3in (68.6cm) gauge, ran into the hills from Machynlleth from 1859, using locomotives from 1878; it was later owned by the GWR and survived briefly into national ownership, being shut down in August 1948. Some of its equipment survives on the Talyllyn line. Another victim of hard times was the Welshpool & Llanfair Railway, of 2ft 6in (76.2cm) gauge, which was opened in 1903 and acquired by the Cambrian; its passenger traffic was terminated by the GWR in 1931, though it ran goods trains until 1956. It has been resuscitated as a tourist line. One narrow-gauge line that never quite closed is the Talyllyn, 2ft 3in (68.5cm), run-ning down from Abergynolwyn to the coast, and the Cambrian line, at Towyn; through the work of many volunteers, it survived the death of its patriarchal owner, Sir Haydn Jones, in 1950 and successfully converted from slate to tourist traffic. The Talyllyn venture became a model for many other preservation attempts.

The same success was achieved by the picturesque Vale of Rheidol line, opened in 1902, from Aberystwyth to Devil's Bridge. Acquired in 1913 by the Cambrian, it was notable at the end of 1968 as the only section of British Railways still to be operated by steam locomotives (it was privatized in 1989). Of purely touristic intention was the highest railway in Great Britain, the 2ft 7½in (80cm) Snowdon Mountain Railway, from Llanberis to the summit at 3540ft (1079m), opened on 6 April 1896. Worked as a rack railway on the Swiss Abt system, its one and only accident was on the very first day, when engine No 1, *Ladas*, jumped the tracks and went over the precipice.

The narrow-gauge steam scene in Wales remains buoyant in the twenty-first cen-tury, with work well in progress to restore the Welsh Highland's line between Porthmadog, Beddgelert and Dinas.

ISLAND RAILWAYS

Apart from Anglesey, which has carried a mainline railway since 1850, the only off-shore islands to have been provided with railways are the Isle of Man and the Isle of

OPPOSITE The romance of steam, of the night train and of the night mail are all captured together as ex-LNER inside-cylinder B12 4-6-0 61572 stands at the canopied platform of Loughborough Central in this atmospheric re-enactment staged in 1998.

Wight. Plans to lay public light railways on Lewis and Skye never got beyond the discussion stage, though short narrow-gauge industrial/military tracks were laid in Orkney and Shetland. A short modern miniature steam line runs on Mull. The Isle of Wight lines were laid to standard gauge, beginning with the Cowes & Newport Railway in July 1862. By 1875, the island's network was complete, and two lines – the Isle of Wight and the Isle of Wight Central – were amalgamated with the LSWR in 1922; the remaining line joined them in the Southern Railway the following year. The Manx lines were built to a 3ft (91.4cm) gauge, like Irish narrow-gauge lines. The first were built by the Isle of Man Railway Company from Douglas to Peel and Douglas to Port Erin in 1873 and 1874, respectively. The Manx Northern joined Ramsey to the Peel–Douglas line via the west side of the island. The Isle of Man Railway was the first in the country to standardize electric lighting in its (admittedly small) stock of carriages. Steam-operated lines survive on both islands, although the original networks are considerably reduced, especially on the Isle of Wight.

PRESERVATION VENTURES

The departure of steam and the closures of lines resulted in many private and voluntary ventures in preservation. The first successful reopening of a closed standard-gauge line was in the Severn Valley in 1959. Local councils, tourist boards and railway enthusiasts sometimes worked in harmony to maintain or re-lay branches that run through attractive countryside and to preserve buildings and equipment of the steam era. Some steam depots, such as Didcot, Tyseley (Birmingham), Carnforth, Barrow Hill at Chesterfield

ABOVE For a time the only part of British Railways still wedded to steam, the Vale of Rheidol line is now privately owned. This forward shot of one of its side-tank locos shows how much overhang a narrow-gauge train can have.

(the last working roundhouse) and Southall, were preserved. A number of industrial lines have also been preserved or restored, one of them running through a still-operative steelworks at Scunthorpe. Not all such ventures flourished, but over 130 steam lines, centres and museums still exist in Britain. Heritage railways are quite a substantial industry in their own right. Even in the era of Railtrack and its successor, seasonal steam trains still run on the West Highland line between Fort William and Mallaig.

Some of the scrap merchants obligingly held off demolition while enthusiasts tried to assemble funds to buy a particular engine. Of the once vast steam stud, only a few

ABOVE The preserved LNER J39 0-6-0, in British Rail paintwork as 65894, re-enacts a typical steam freight working, on the North Yorkshire Moors Railway, in 1996. The class dates from 1926, and most of the locomotives were built at Darlington Works.

LEFT O.V.S. Bulleid's class Q1 0-6-0 of the Southern Railway carried the wartime 'Austerity' look almost to the point of self-parody. On a crisp February morning in 2000, the preserved No 33001 heads the 9.15 a.m. to Kingscote on the Bluebell Railway.

dozen still survive, but they cover a considerable range of years and types. Among the real veterans, remarkably, they include *Rocket* and the even earlier colliery engine *Puffing Billy* (1813) at London's Science Museum; and the equally old *Wylam Dilly* in the Museum of Scotland, Edinburgh. Kent's first engine, *Invicta*, survives at Canterbury. Two Stockton & Darlington engines are preserved, *Locomotion* and *Derwent*. The Liverpool & Manchester's *Lion* of 1838 survives, as does Crewe's first engine, *Columbine*, and a Bury 0-4-0, nicknamed *Coppernob*, of the Furness Railway. The record-breakers *City of Truro* and *Mallard* can still be seen, at the Swindon and York railway museums respectively. Engines which caught the public's imagination were most likely to be chosen, and several 'Castles' and A4s were preserved. Many other types survive in unique examples. No broad-gauge engine has survived, though the GWR retained two until 1905. Battles to preserve historic types go back to the 1930s at least, when public outcry saved the Caledonian single No 123, the LNWR 'Jumbo' *Hardwicke* and the GWR *City of Truro* from the indifference or even hostility of railway officials. The LNER was the only one of the Big Four to have any proper care for its own heritage.

At one time it might have been thought that the urge to preserve steam trains would not survive the generation which had grown up with them. But the popularity of steam lines and steam centres is as strong as ever. Many have plans for extension of their lines and services. Increasingly, the visitors who come have never known the days when the steam locomotive was the most visible, exciting and essential feature of railway life.

ABOVE Steaming bravely into a new dawn – ex-British Railways 9F 2-10-0 takes the first train of the day, year and century out of Loughborough Central for Leicester, Great Central Railway, on 1 January 2000.

TIME LINE OF THE BRITISH STEAM RAILWAY

1804
Richard Trevithick successfully demonstrates a steam railway engine, for the first time in the world, at Penydarren, Wales, 22 February.

1813
William Hedley builds *Puffing Billy* and *Wylam Dilly* as colliery locomotives.

1815
George Stephenson invents the blast system, driving exhaust steam from the cylinders through the boiler to the chimney.

1825
Opening of Stockton & Darlington Railway, 27 September.

George Stephenson builds *Locomotion*, the first engine with coupled wheels.

1829
George Stephenson constructs the *Rocket* 0-2-2 locomotive.

Rainhill locomotive trials are held, 6–14 October. *Rocket* is the winner.

1830
The *Planet* 2-2-0 locomotive type is introduced, among the first to have inside cylinders beneath the smokebox.

1833
First British bogie engines (0-2-4) run on the Dundee & Newtyle Railway.

1840
First locomotive roundhouse is built at Derby (Midland Railway).

1843
The Grand Junction locomotive works are transferred from Edge Hill, Liverpool, to Crewe.

Swindon Works (GWR) opens on 2 January. The LSWR begins to build its own engines at Nine Elms.

1845
Crewe Works produces its first locomotive, *Columbine*.

1846
Gauge Commission reports against extension of the broad gauge.

Swindon's first engine, *Great Western*, is built.

1850
The brick-arch firebox, to facilitate coal burning, is developed on the Midland Railway between 1850 and 1859.

1851
J E McConnell introduces his 2-2-2 class (LNWR), known as the 'Bloomers'.

Stratford Works, Eastern Counties Railway, builds its first engine.

1853
The Great Northern sets up its locomotive works at Doncaster.

1856
John Ramsbottom (LNWR) introduces his 'foolproof' safety valve and the screw reverser.

The Caledonian Railway opens its works at St Rollox, Glasgow.

GNR express 4-2-2 1004, built in 1895.

1859
The steam injector is developed by the French engineer Henri Giffard and is rapidly taken up in Britain.

1860
First water troughs installed, by John Ramsbottom, on the LNWR Chester & Holyhead line.

Between 1860 and 1863 Alfred Jules Belpaire, Belgian engineer, develops his flat-topped firebox, used by many British locomotive designers.

1863
Steam engines replace horses on the Festiniog Railway (opened 1836).

1864
John Fowler's 'Metropolitan' 4-4-0T is introduced for underground running.

Robert Fairlie patents his double-bogie articulated locomotive design.

1866
William Stroudley develops three sizes of locomotive-mounted snowplough (HR).

1869
Fairlie double-ended engine first used, on the Festiniog line.

1870
The first of Patrick Stirling's 8ft (243.8cm) bogie singles, 4-2-2, is built, for the GNR.

1871
The first inside-cylinder, inside-frame 4-4-0 express type is built by Thomas Wheatley for the NBR.

1874
F W Webb's 'Jumbo' class 2-4-0 is introduced (LNWR); the first is called *Precedent*.
James Stirling introduces steam reversing gear (GSWR).

Stephenson's 0-2-2 Northumbrian of 1830.

1876

Crewe Works builds its 2,000th locomotive. First British use of the Walschaerts valve gear, developed in Belgium by Egide Walschaerts in 1844, is on an 0-6-6-0 Fairlie locomotive of the East & West Junction Railway.

1878

The GER introduces the first British outside-cylinder 2-6-0 Mogul engines.

Corris narrow-gauge railway (opened 1859) acquires locomotives.

1880

F W Webb's 'Cauliflower' 0-6-0 class is introduced (LNWR).

Class 4 'BR standard' 4-6-0 75069.

1885

William Stroudley introduces the *Gladstone* 0-4-2 class (LBSCR).

1886

The Barry Railway introduces the first British 0-8-0 type, with outside cylinders.

1887

Crewe Works builds its 3,000th locomotive.

1888

'Races' from London to Edinburgh reduce journey time to 7 hours 45 minutes.

1892

All remaining broad-gauge lines are narrowed to standard between March and May; last broad-gauge passenger trains run on 20 May.

1894

David Jones introduces the 'Big Goods', first 4-6-0 to run in Britain (HR).

1895

'Races' from London to Aberdeen this summer reduce journey times to a minimum 8 hours 32 minutes (East Coast) and 8 hours 38 minutes (West Coast) on 22 August.

Ex-LMS 'Jinty' class 3F 0-6-0T, at the Midland Railway Centre.

1896

J G McIntosh introduces the big-boilered 4-4-0 *Dunalastair* class.

1898

H A Ivatt builds Britain's first Atlantic type 4-4-2, *Henry Oakley* (GNR).

1899

Wilson Worsdell builds the first express 4-6-0 engines to run in Britain (NER).

Dugald Drummond introduces the T9 class 4-4-0, nicknamed 'Greyhounds' (LSWR).

Sir John Aspinall introduces his 'Highflyer' inside-cylinder 4-4-2 type (L&YR).

1900

'Claud Hamilton' 4-4-0 class introduced on the GER.

Wainwright/Surtees 'D' class 4-4-0 introduced on the SE&C.

1901

H A Ivatt builds his first large-boilered Atlantic, No 251 (GNR), also the 'Long Tom' 0-8-0 for coal trains.

1902

The Midland Railway builds its first three-cylinder compound 4-4-0 for express passenger work.

Stratford Works, GER, builds the 'Decapod' 0-10-0 tank.

LNWR 'Jumbo' 2-4-0 *Charles Dickens* completes 2,000,000 miles (3,218,600km) of running since 1882.

Restored GWR 4-4-0 City of Truro at Swindon.

1903

G J Churchward builds the first British 2-8-0 goods types (GWR) and introduces the 'City' class 4-4-0.

LBSC class B4 4-4-0 No 70 establishes a steam-power record for Victoria–Brighton, 48 minutes 41 seconds, 26 July.

1904

102.3mph (164.6km/h) is claimed for 4-4-0 *City of Truro* (GWR) on the 'Ocean Mail', between Plymouth and Bristol, 9 May.

George Whale introduces the *Precursor* class 4-4-0 (LNWR).

1905

Deeley introduces his modification of the Johnson-Smith compound 4-4-0 with MR No 1000.

Steam running in the London Underground tunnels is phased out.

1906

J F McIntosh introduces the *Cardean* class express 4-6-0 (CR).

W P Reid introduces his Atlantic class express 4-4-2 (NBR).

1907

G J Churchward introduces the four-cylinder 'Star' and two-cylinder 'Saint' class 4-6-0 types (GWR).

R M Deeley's first 4-4-0 compounds appear on the Midland.

A record non-stop run for Wales is made between Cardiff and Fishguard (GWR), 120 miles (193km), on 15 August.

1908

Churchward builds Britain's first Pacific, *The Great Bear,* the GWR's only 4-6-2 (later converted to 4-6-0).

D Earle Marsh applies the Schmidt super-heater to express engines: the I.3 4-4-2 tank.

1909

The MR begins to extend centralized traffic control throughout its sytem.

Class J31 0-6-0 Maude, at Bo'ness.

1911

D Earle Marsh's superheated Atlantics are introduced on the LBSCR.

Sir Vincent Raven's Z-class Atlantics are introduced on the NER.

C J Bowen-Cooke's superheated 'Prince of Wales' 4-6-0s are introduced on the LNWR.

Dugald Drummond's 'Paddlebox' express 4-6-0s are introduced on the LSWR.

J G Robinson introduces his 2-8-0 goods engine (GCR); this will be the standard ROD military engine of the First World War.

1913

Bowen-Cooke introduces the 'Claughton' class 4-6-0 (LNWR).

R H Whitelegg builds the first British 4-6-4 express tank engines (London Tilbury & Southend Railway).

J G Robinson's 'Director' class express 4-4-0s are introduced on the Great Central.
W P Reid's 'Glen' 4-4-0 class is introduced (NBR).

British companies own 22,267 locomotives, of which 10,600 are 0-6-0 or 0-6-0T.

1914

First locomotives to be built in Germany for British use: 10 Borsig 4-4-0s to R E L Maunsell's design for the SE&CR.

1922

The first Gresley Pacific, Class A1 *Great Northern,* is constructed by the Great Northern.

1923

The first GWR 'Castle' four-cylinder 4-6-0, *Caerphilly Castle,* is built at Swindon.

The total number of steam locomotives in service reaches 23,963.

1924

Gresley's three-cylinder K3 express freight 2-6-0 is introduced: heaviest eight-wheeler British locomotive.

1925

Gresley's 'Garratt' type 2-8-0+0-8-2 is introduced for banking duties in the Yorkshire coalfield.

Maunsell's two-cylinder 'King Arthur' express 4-6-0s are introduced on the Southern.

1926

Maunsell introduces the four-cylinder 'Lord Nelson' class express 4-6-0 on the Southern.

1927

C B Collett introduces the 'King' class 4-6-0, *King George V,* claimed as most powerful express locomotive in the country (GWR).

The LMS introduces the 'Royal Scot' class 4-6-0; also a 2-6-0+0-6-2 'Garratt' type for heavy freight.

First British use of blinkers on locomotives to lift smoke away from the boiler, on the SR.

1928

Gresley introduces the A3 'Super-Pacific' on the LNER; also the corridor tender to enable non-stop running from London to Edinburgh, longest in the world; the first run is on 1 May with the 10am 'Flying Scotsman', drawn by A1 Pacific *Flying Scotsman.*

1930

Maunsell's 'Schools' class three-cylinder 4-4-0 is introduced on the Southern.

The 'Patriot' or 'Baby Scot' lighter version of the 'Royal Scot' 4-6-0 is introduced on the LMS.

Gresley's experimental high-pressure 4-6-2 No 10000 is built as a one-off.

1931

Launceston Castle on the 'Cheltenham Flyer' makes world record start-to-stop journey speed, 79.5mph (128km/h) from Swindon to Paddington, 16 September.

1932

Tregenna Castle improves on the 1931 record with an average speed of 81.7mph (131.4km/h).

1933

William Stanier builds the first LMS Pacific, *The Princess Royal.*

1934

First scientifically confirmed speed of over 100mph (160.9km/h) by a steam locomotive is attained by A1 Pacific 4472 *Flying Scotsman* (LNER) on 30 November.

Stanier introduces the 'Black Five' 4-6-0 mixed-traffic locomotive (LMS), also the 'Jubilee' express 4-6-0.

Gresley introduces the first P2 class 2-8-2 express locomotive for the Edinburgh–Aberdeen route, *Cock o' the North;* class later rebuilt as A2/2 Pacifics (LNER).

1935

Gresley's A4 class streamlined Pacific is introduced (LNER); the first is 2509 *Silver Link.*

Stanier's 'Coronation' class streamlined Pacific is introduced (LMS); the 'turbomotive' 4-6-2 No 6202 is built as a one-off.

A3 Pacific 2750 *Papyrus* attains 108mph (173.8km/h) on a test run, LNER, 5 March.

A4 Pacific *Silver Link* twice attains 112.5mph (181km/h) on a demonstration run, LNER, 27 September.

The LNER runs the 'Silver Jubilee' London–Newcastle 4-hour express from 27 September.

1936

Gresley's V2 class express freight 2-6-2 is introduced on the LNER.

Last double-frame engines are built, the 4-4-0 'Dukedogs' of the GWR.

1937

The LMS reduces minimum London–Glasgow journey time from 7 1/2 hours to 6 1/2 with the *Coronation Scot.*

LMS streamlined Pacific 6230 *Coronation* reaches 114mph (183.4km/h) approaching Crewe, 29 June.

1938

LNER class A4 Pacific *Mallard* establishes world speed record for steam locomotives of 126mph (202.8km/h), 3 July.

Stanier's 'Duchess' Pacific class is introduced.

Two match-wagons separate LMS 8F 0-8-0 49119 from its tank train.

1939

LMS Pacific 6234 *Duchess of Abercorn* produces highest recorded power output for a British steam locomotive: 3,300 indicated horsepower.

1941

The first Bulleid air-smoothed 'Merchant Navy' Pacific is introduced.

5035 Coity Castle heading the 'Bristolian'.

1942

O V S Bulleid introduces the Q1 class 0-6-0 (SR).

1943

Edward Thompson's LNER B1 class 4-6-0 is introduced.

Rebuilding of the LMS 'Royal Scot' 4-6-0s begins, with improved performance resulting.

The LNER P2 2-8-2s are rebuilt as A2/2 Pacifics.

1944

Thompson's A2/1 Pacifics are introduced (LNER).

1945

A H Peppercorn introduces his A1 Pacific (LNER).

O V S Bulleid introduces the 'West Country' and 'Battle of Britain' light Pacifics (SR).

1946

Edward Thompson's final Pacific design, class A2, is introduced (LNER); the first is announced as Doncaster Works' 2,000th locomotive.

1947

A H Peppercorn's A2 Pacific is introduced (LNER).

O V S Bulleid begins work on the 'Leader' bogie-driven general-purpose tank locomotive (later abandoned).

British companies own 19,843 locomotives; 7,240 are 0-6-0 or 0-6-0T; 279 are Pacifics.

1948

Peppercorn's A1 Pacific is introduced (LNE Region).

Opening of the steam locomotive testing plant at Rugby, 19 October.

Interregional locomotive trials are staged.

1951

BR Standard 'Britannia' 4-6-2 locomotive introduced; also the class 4 mixed-traffic 4-6-0.

1954

Transport Modernization Plan envisages phasing-out of steam traction.

The class 9F 2-10-0 freight locomotive is introduced.

1955

A top speed of 107mph (172.2km/h) is claimed for 'King' class 4-6-0 6015 *King Richard III* (Western Region) near Lavington, September.

1956

The Clean Air Act requires the minimizing of smoke emission from railway engines.

1957

City of Truro is restored to main-line running order and achieves 84mph (135km/h) on a 280-ton (284.5-tonne) special working.

1958

The last Atlantic 4-4-2 in regular service (ex-LBSC) is withdrawn.

Construction at Crewe of its last main-line steam locomotive for Britain, Class 9F 2-10-0 92250, the 7,331st engine built there.

British Railways owns 16,108 steam locomotives.

1960

BR's last steam engine, 9F 2-10-0 92220, built at Swindon, is named *Evening Star*.

1961

Last steam service on the Metropolitan Line of London Transport, 9 September.

1963

A4 Pacific 60007 *Sir Nigel Gresley* on a special train reaches 103mph (165.8km/h) at Essendine.

British Railways ownership of steam locomotives is down to 7,050.

1964

'Merchant Navy' Pacific 35005 reaches 100mph (160.9km/h) near Winchester on the 21.20 Waterloo–Bournemouth, April 28.

A3 Pacific 60106 *Flying Fox* reaches 100mph (160.9km/h) at Essendine on a Gresley Society special, 2 May.

1965

Last regular steam service from Paddington ends, 27 November, pulled by *Clun Castle*.

1966

Steam services discontinued between Euston, Liverpool and Manchester.

1968

From 8 August, steam traction is withdrawn from British Rail.

By December, British Rail has only three steam locomotives in operation, on the Vale of Rheidol narrow-gauge line in Wales.

Stanier Pacific 46257 City of Salford at speed with the 'Caledonian'.

GLOSSARY

ATC: Automatic train control system.

Abt system: A rack-and-pinion track with two adjacent toothed racks between the rails, the teeth placed in staggered positions; used on the Snowdon Mountain Railway.

Adhesion: The ability of a locomotive to pull without slipping on the rails.

Atlantic: A 4-4-2 engine, so called from the Atlantic Coast Line in the USA, which first built them.

Axle load: The weight placed on the track by a pair of wheels with an axle between them.

Ballast: The materials, usually stone chips, on which the railway track is laid.

Baltic: A 4-6-4 tank locomotive.

Banking: The use of one or more engines to help push a train up a gradient, or 'bank'.

Bogie: A wheeled undercarriage for an engine or railway vehicle, pivoted to allow it to turn independently.

Boiler: The long metal barrel, filled with tubes for water, steam and fire exhaust, in which steam is generated by means of the firebox situated at one end.

Boiler pressure: The maximum pressure – expressed in pounds per square inch (psi) or kilogram per square centimetre (kg/cm2) – of steam within the boiler before the safety valve opens to release excessive pressure.

Caprotti valve gear: A valve gear driven by a rotating shaft rather than by rods and levers.

Carrying wheels: The non-coupled wheels of a locomotive.

Clerestory: A central raised section of carriage roof, often with ventilators and window lights let into the side panels.

Composite carriage: A coach incorporating more than one class of accommodation; or a combined passenger coach and guard's van.

Connecting rod: The rod joining the driving axle crank to the piston rod via the cross-head.

Consolidation: A 2-8-0 locomotive; the term is rarely used in Britain.

Coupled wheels: Engine wheels joined by coupling rods.

Crank: An arm attached to an axle or rotating spindle, with a rod attached at right angles to the crank axle.

Crossover: A piece of track enabling trains to move from one line on to a parallel line.

Cut-off: 1) A term used to express the amount of steam admitted to the cylinder, in relation to the position of the piston. 2) A section of line built to bypass a station or circuitous length of route.

Cylinder: The part of the engine where the drive is generated; the power of steam is converted into motion by pushing the piston.

Dome: A feature of most but not all locomotives, normally holding the steam collection pipe controlled by the regulator.

Double chimney: A locomotive chimney with two exhaust blast-pipes inside; the

'Black 5' 45474 takes on water at Achnashellach.

form most common being the Kylchap double-blast exhaust.

Double heading: The use of two engines to pull a train.

Down: The direction leading away from the major terminus of the line; hence down line, down train, etc.

Driving wheels: Engine wheels driven from the cylinders.

Facing points: Points which a train meets when travelling forwards.

Footplate: The cab floor on which the enginemen stand, linking engine and tender.

Frame: 1) The structure of a locomotive, resting on the axles, that supports the boiler. It may be inside the wheels or outside them, or, in the case of a double fame, between them. 2) An interlocking set of tracks and signals, controlled by levers.

Gauge: The width between the rails.

Injector: A device for forcing water from the tank into the boiler; it can be driven by live steam or by exhaust steam that has already passed through the cylinders.

Limited: Used of trains, it means an express with limited accommodation, which should be booked in advance.

Mikado: A 2-8-2 locomotive.

Mixed train: A train with both passenger and goods vehicles.

Mogul: A 2-6-0 locomotive.

Off: A signal is 'off' when it indicates a clear road.

On: A signal is 'on' when it indicates stop.

Pacific: A 4-6-2 locomotive.

Pilot engine: Usually the front and smaller engine of a double-headed train; but on some lines, eg the West Highland, the pilot was the second engine.

Points: The system of movable rails, controlled by a points lever, enabling tracks to merge with each other.

Pony wheels: The trailing wheels of certain locomotive types, eg Atlantics.

Power classification: A notation devised by the LMS and used also by British Railways, with numerals broadly grading the power of locomotives from 1 up to 10; and letters specifying type of traffic: P (passenger), F (freight), MT (mixed traffic).

Prairie: A 2-6-2 locomotive; the term is rarely used in Britain.

Pullman: A luxury carriage built for and leased by the Pullman Car Company.

Rake: A line of coaches coupled together.

Regulator: The device controlling the flow of steam from the boiler to the cylinders; one of the key driving instruments.

Reverser: The device that sets the valve gear for forward or reverse motion.

Route availability: A code used by the LNER and other lines, sometimes painted on engine cab sides. Consisting of the letters RA and a numeral, it indicated the range of lines an engine was allowed to run on.

Running powers: The permission, for an agreed fee, to run trains on a track belonging to another company.

Safety valve: An automatic valve which opens to release steam if the boiler pressure exceeds the boiler's maximum operating pressure.

Sandwich frame: A type of locomotive frame in which wood (first oak, later teak) was used, with thin metal plates on each side.

Sleeper: 1) The transverse wooden or concrete slab supporting the track. 2) A carriage fitted with sleeping compartments, or a train of such carriages.

Slip coach: A carriage which could be detached from the rear of a moving train and, controlled by a brakeman, be allowed to coast to a halt in the station.

Tank engine: A locomotive carrying its coal and water supply within its own frame: no tender.

Tractive effort: Usually expressed in pounds (or kilograms) as 'nominal tractive effort', it is worked out by a mathematical formula to establish the theoretical backward push exerted on the rail by the driving wheels with the locomotive in full gear and with maximum boiler pressure, assuming no friction anywhere other than between wheels and rail.

Trailing wheels: Wheels of a locomotive positioned to the rear of the coupled wheels.

Up: The direction leading towards the major terminus of the line; hence up line, up train, etc.

Valve gear: The arrangement of rods and cranks controlling admission of steam to the cylinders.

Wheel arrangement: A standard notation for describing steam locomotives, known as Whyte's after its deviser, in which the number of driving or coupled wheels is placed in the centre, and that of leading and trailing wheels before and after respectively. Thus an engine with no leading wheels, six coupled wheels and two trailing wheels is an 0-6-2. If a tank engine, it is an 0-6-2T.

BIBLIOGRAPHY

Ahrons, E L, *British Steam Locomotives, 1825–1925*. London, 1927

Burton, Anthony, and Scott-Morgan, John, *Britain's Light Railways*. Ashbourne, 1985

Clay, John F (ed), *Essays in Steam*. Shepperton, 1970

Cooper, B K, *Great Western Railway Handbook*. London, 1986

Ellis, C H, *British Railway History* (2 vols). London, 1954–59

Ellis, C H, *Some Classic Locomotives*. London, 1949

Ferneyhough, Frank, *The History of Railways in Britain*. London, 1975

Grinling, C H, *The Great Northern Railway*. London, 1898

Lloyd, Roger, *Railwaymen's Gallery*. London, 1953

Nock, O S, *British Steam Locomotives at Work*. London, 1967

Nock, O S, *Steam Locomotive* (2nd ed). London, 1968

Nock, O S, *Rail, Steam and Speed*. London, 1970

Reed, Brian, *Modern Locomotive Classes*. London, 1945

Richard, J, and MacKenzie, J M, *The Railway Station: A Social History*. Oxford, 1986

Simmons, Jack, *The Railway in Town and Country, 1830–1914*. Newton Abbot, 2000

Tuplin, W A, *British Steam Since 1900*. Newton Abbot, 1969

INDEX

PICTURE CREDITS